January

For Linton –
A book that yes
as a true Chicagoan
will appreciate – enjoy!

MY LIFE
A Conversational Memoir

Joseph D. Feaney

MY LIFE

A Conversational Memoir

Mary Jane Kearney

MARQUETTE
UNIVERSITY
PRESS

Library of Congress Cataloguing in Publication Data
Kearney, Mary Jane, 1930-1997
My life : a conversational memoir / Mary Jane Kearney.
p. cm.
Includes bibliographical references (p.   ) and index.
ISBN 0-87462-010-4 (pbk. : alk. paper)
1. Kearney, Mary Jane, 1930-1997. 2. College teachers—United States—Biography. I. Title.
LA2317.K28 A3 2001
378.1'2'092—dc21
2001006104

© 2001. All rights reserved. No part of this publication may be reproduced, stored in a retrieval system, or transmitted in any form or by any means, electronic, mechanical, photocopying, recording, or other, without permission in writing of the family of Mary Jane Kearney, except for quotation of brief passages in scholarly books, articles, and reviews. Address inquiries to Post Office Box 2145, Milwaukee, Wisconsin 53201-2145.

MARQUETTE UNIVERSITY PRESS
MILWAUKEE

The Association of Jesuit University Presses

CONTENTS

	EDITOR'S INTRODUCTION	xi
	PREFACE	xiii
	PART ONE	
I	THE WORLD I CAME FROM	3
II	GIFTS IN THE R.S.G. TRADITION: USEFUL AND LOVING	7
III	THE ST. LOUIS CONNECTION AND THE GRANDFATHER WHO WAS MY "PAL"	10
IV	HOW I DISCOVERED THE REAL WORLD: THE LOOP AND MARSHALL FIELD'S	13
V	MOTHER	16
VI	THE NEIGHBORHOOD—OUR LOST AMERICA	19
VII	MORE NEIGHBORHOOD VIGNETTES: FAITH AND HOPE TRANSPLANTED	22
VIII	DIAMOND LAKE— MY CHILDHOOD GARDEN OF EDEN	26
IX	AUNT BESSIE AND UNCLE JOE	29
X	CATHERINE AND OTHERS	33
XI	FAMILY MEMORIES	37
XII	ADOLESCENT UNCERTAINTIES: FINDING AND USING ONE'S STRENGTHS	40
XIII	OUR WORLD: A RETROSPECTIVE	44
XIV	LONGWOOD AND LIBERATION	47

v

XV	A THANKSGIVING WITH DOROTHY	51
XVI	THE MARQUETTE MOMENT	54
XVII	LOYOLA	58
XVIII	THE REMARKABLE AUNT MARY	62
XIX	MAYBE TEACHING: AN EXPLORATORY FORAY	66
XX	IRELAND AND LONGWOOD	70
XXI	A LAST GLANCE AT ETHNICITY AND IRISH CATHOLICISM	74
XXII	THE CYO DETOUR	77
XXIII	ST. XAVIER	81
XXIV	PROVIDENCE: COURTSHIP AND ENGAGEMENT	86
XXV	THE FEAST OF ST. ANNE: JULY 26, 1958	91
XXVI	STARTING OUT	94
XXVII	BEGINNINGS	97
XXVIII	MARY KATE	100
XXIX	DAD'S DEATH	103
XXX	EARLY YEARS OF PARENTING AND EDMUND	106
XXXI	TRANSITIONS	111
XXXII	OAKLEY HOUSE, JOHN'S ARRIVAL, AND THE LOSS OF A MOTHER	115
XXXIII	JOSEPH	120
XXXIV	THE 1960S: A FAMILY A' BUILDING	123
XXXV	ROBERT	128

Contents vii

XXXVI	THE MIDDLE YEARS—FAMILY AND PROFESSION	133
	EDITOR'S POSTSCRIPT— LIVING, LOVING, AND PARTING, 1990-1997	137

PART TWO

	EDITOR'S NOTE— MUSINGS, VIGNETTES, AND ESSAYS	168
I	THE MOST UNFORGETTABLE CHARACTER I'VE MET (CA. 1948)	169
II	REMEMBRANCES OF A PRACTICAL GIVER (CA. 1991)	172
III	A MOTHER LEFT HOLDING THE BAG	174
IV	ON BOYS, BOUDOIRS, AND BOOBIES	176
V	ON THE ENJOYMENT OF THE MUNDANE: AN OCTOBER MORNING	177
VI	REFLECTIONS ON MUTUAL PILGRIMAGES	179
VII	A WORLD PROGRAMMED TO SAY "NO!"	180
VIII	FIFTY YEARS LATER	182
IX	WE ALWAYS GO TO BED ANGRY	185
X	MISTY: A FOND REMEMBRANCE	187
XI	RESCUING FAMILY HERITAGE	189
XII	ANOTHER VIEW OF FOREIGN CAB DRIVERS	191
XIII	MODERN WOMAN	194
XIV	CHILDHOOD AND TV'S REAL VIOLENCE: THE END OF CONVERSATION	196
XV	ST. VALENTINE KNEW WE NEEDED HIM	198

XVI	THE ART OF THE UNFINISHED	201
XVII	THE BACK TO SCHOOL PARTY	203
XVIII	PROTOTYPE LETTER TO AN INDEPENDENT YOUNG ADULT AWAY IN COLLEGE	204
XIX	THOUGHTS ON DELIVERING A SON—TO COLLEGE	205
XX	ON OUR NEED FOR SILENCE, OR RECONSIDERING HAMLET	207
XXI	A THOROUGHLY MODERN "MODEST PROPOSAL"	209
XXII	THOUGHTS ON TAKING DOWN THE HOLIDAY DECORATIONS	211
XXIII	SOME THOUGHTS ON MULTI-CULTURALISM AND CHILDREN'S READINGS	212
XXIV	CABBAGE PATCH MANIA REVEALS SOCIETY SHIFT	215
XXV	BROKEN WRIST A REAL ICE-BREAKER	217
XXVI	MOM AND POP ROBIN— THE IDEAL SUMMER VISITORS	219
XXVII	NO WONDER MANY TEACHERS-TO-BE FALL SHORT	221
XXVIII	SOME THINGS IN LIFE—AND AT NOTRE DAME— KEEP REPEATING	224
XXIX	AT LEAST TEN REASONS FOR THE TIRED TEACHER TO ANSWER THE SCHOOL BELL	227
XXX	RULES FOR TEACHERS	232
XXXI	IRELAND: 1953	234
XXXII	MARGE CALLAHAN AT PLAY	240
XXXIII	DEAR TEACHER	246

ACKNOWLEDGMENT

Selected material is reprinted from the Sonnets of Hilaire Belloc with the permission of the Belloc literary estate.

Children for memory : the Faith for pride :
Good land to leave : and young Love satisfied.

Hilaire Belloc, *Sonnet XVI*

Editor's Introduction

Over the years, Mary Jane wrote for her own enjoyment and to provide partial answers to the questions of her grandchildren (and she hoped beyond them) as to "Who am I?" and "Where did I come from?" She chose to call her writings "Recollections." She avoided the term "Memoirs" as pretentious. Laughingly, she said that perhaps a variation on Mary McCarthy's *Memories of a Catholic Girlhood* might be in order—something like *Recollections of a Generally Happy Catholic Girlhood*. In a letter to her cousin Martha, Mary Jane defined her intent in these writings. She was sending Martha a couple of chapters from "my memoirs." She wrote as follows: "That is a highfalutin' term for my recollections of what it was like to grow up Irish and Catholic and a member of this family in the '30s and '40s. . . . I do it as much for my own satisfaction and enjoyment of memory as anything, but I justify it as something to leave for my own kids. When my father died when Mary Kate was just a month old, and my mother five years later, I realized that the children's memories would be almost nothing. Ed and I promised each other we would not let them die in our kids' minds. I think my kids think they know R.S.G. because every now and then one of the boys will say, 'I'm like Grandpa Grogan . . . .' Naturally, it tickles me."

Actually, the unedited copy she presented to us was simply titled "My Life." That comes closest to her intent. This was not intended to be a "My Life and Times." Her intent was to write a personal, not a reflective, narrative, although at some points her observations on modern society break through. Her life was family, friends, books, and students. She was interested in political and social affairs, but they were not the centrality of her existence. She would create a better world but primarily by focusing on what, to her, was life's ultimate purpose—simply serving God by serving the needs of those He had given to her care.

So this is her story. At many points there is an overlapping of content both within her recollections (which form Part One of this book), since she wrote them over an extended period, and also between them and her other writings and essays (which I have included as Part Two). I thought it best to leave all of this undisturbed. Her intent was not to produce something that was a highly polished "seamless web" but more as she once said "a conversation" intended for those who wanted to listen. If all of the typos have not been caught, if the finished editing is a shade short of professional, I can only repeat Mary Jane's oft-stated Aristotelian urging: Get moving. "Don't let the best be the enemy of the good."

The excerpts from Hilaire Belloc that frame the manuscript are my addition. They are of a personal nature and they, too, were part of her life.

Edmund W. Kearney
Chicago 2001

Preface

My youngest son, a poet at heart but a lawyer by training, says I am to be the story-teller who builds a bridge, which two generations who have never met can cross to come to know each other. His charge recalls to me my conviction of how important it is to tell children stories of the lives of their parents and grandparents.

Here then is my story. The accounts range from my father giving away whistling teakettles for the sale of concrete garbage boxes set in Chicago alleys in the 1920s to his manner of hiring employees by parking his car in front of employment agencies until he saw a face he found interesting and suggestive of character. They run a gamut of family memories from childhood trips to Maxwell Street through marriage and children to the 1990s.

So in the spirit of past whistling teakettles, here are some bricks of the bridge by which we of this generation can speak to those on the far side of the span.

Mary Jane Kearney
Chicago 1995

PART ONE

I
THE WORLD I CAME FROM

One of the earliest memories of my father's business, the Chicago Granitine Manufacturing Company, dating back to the middle '30s, was his offering whistling teakettles as a premium to accompany the purchase of concrete laundry tubs ("with built-in washboard") and alley-opening garbage boxes. Admittedly not an exciting market—perhaps he felt that something a little more "gimmicky" like this relatively new device of whistling teakettles would be a selling feature in the Depression-racked U.S.A., to which Chicago was no exception.

I don't know how successful this sales campaign was, monetarily, but the business survived another thirty years, when it finally succumbed to the onslaught of plastics and other synthetics. The '30s must have been a hard time for the company as it was for business generally, but at home we never felt the difference. Nor did we feel it positively in the immediate post-war era when there was so much building. To have spent more money then, just because it was there, would have been a scandal to my parents' philosophy, which was that of second-generation Irish-Americans whose parents had come over in one of the big immigration periods of the 1870s. If you were not suffering, my parents reasoned, there certainly were people who were, and one didn't have to look far to find them—and help them!

As for our family, there never was a question of money being there for school books or an allowance to cover purchases for my brother's stamp collection or for the many worthy causes whose requests came in one of the two mail deliveries daily. I used to wonder if my father had a "payday," a word often used by the children at our parochial school when they spoke of when they could buy their books. To my parents, discretionary income, as the term is used today, was to "share, save, and spend," in that order, and one never disputed the priorities—or didn't broadcast it if he did.

Dad had become president of the Chicago Granitine Manufacturing Company at twenty-seven (in 1921), just ten years after he had been hired. Mr. Washic, the kind Bohemian man who was his boss, died of blood poisoning after injuring himself on a rusty nail at work. Antitetanus was not in wide usage until considerably later. Chicago Granitine was a small company, with three or four people in the office and forty men in the adjacent factory. My dad, hired fresh out of business college on St. Patrick's Day, and in "short pants," knew every aspect of the business by 1921. He was, from then on, chief executive, sales manager, and personnel director.

Many years later he told me that to get new workers he would drive to an employment agency located in storefronts everywhere in those hard times and study the faces of the men standing in line outside. When he saw a face he liked, he would invite the man into the car to be interviewed and, if that went well, hire him. Perhaps such a practice does not reflect the latest theory of fair employment practices, but it was true to my father's deep and abiding concern for the whole person. You can also be sure that his questions centered on family during the interview, for my father was interested in everything about people. I learned many years later that a sick child or a brother-in-law who needed a job was often the subject of later conversations with his employees and of action, if my father found he could help.

This business and his family became my father's whole thrust. Before his marriage at thirty-two he had been president of every organization in "the French Church," St. John the Baptist at 51st and Peoria Streets. Less fashionable than Visitation, the large parish "on the boulevard" (55th), St. John's needed his expertise and dedicated service managing fund drives and running carnivals. A little pocket of ethnic Chicago history, this parish had clergy representing the two groups residing there—Irish and French—Father Kelly and Father Gelinas, and they ministered equally to their first and second-generation American congregation. But when my father married, all that stopped. It wasn't that he was no longer interested, but the business occupied all of his available time and strength and he wanted the rest for his family. However, a parish solicitor was never turned from our door without an ample donation; neither were the sweating black-clad missionaries who often visited on summer afternoons, with pictures of their "little Indians" or Chinese babies. These put us in touch with the part of the world unknown in pre-television America and made us feel responsible.

But signs of the Depression were everywhere, even to a child not suffering in the '30s. At the end of our block, new curbs and sidewalks were being installed, courtesy of the WPA, and at least once a week, a tramp or "bum," as they were called, would mount the steps to our wooden back porch where my mother would serve him a lunch or supper of leftovers from the night before. She had been instructed, of course, not to allow him in to use the bathroom if he asked, for a woman in her house was then, as now, vulnerable. There was a gas station at the corner, my father said, for those needs. But I never remember the feeling of being really "threatened" as people do today when someone mounts the stairway and knocks on their door. It was just generally accepted that many people were out of work and those of us who had full larders were supposed to assist them. An uncle, my mother's brother, who traveled in his work, would occasionally stop in Chicago to see us, and he told almost unbelievable stories of groups of kids, some as young as ten, whom he would see along the road, making camp and sticking together for mutual support. As I grew up and read more accounts of Depression times, I realized that mine had been a kind of halcyon existence, growing up in the stable middle-class neighborhood, two blocks from State's Attorney Courtney's guarded house, and punctuated by the regular comings and goings of my at times strict and at other times incredibly funny father, and my sympathetic mother who loved our school friends and said "oh Bob" only when he came out with one of his lower digestive tract allusions.

Following one's religion, getting an education, and, if you were a Grogan, doing well at it were important things in life. A corollary was helping others when they were in need. At my father's wake in 1960, just four weeks after my daughter's birth, I heard a number of stories of my father's assisting with a rent check (or probably an envelope of cash in those days) when there was need in a family, or hiring a man to come and shovel snow or sweep up around the office or factory even when it was a nuisance to have him around. It was considered demeaning to just give a handout to a man. My father never considered himself far from that man and the kinship was mutual as illustrated by the affectionate memories shared at his wake.

II
Gifts in the R.S.G. Tradition: Useful and Loving

Gifts were a little different in our family from those given in some of my friends' houses. To my father, Robert Stephen Grogran, or R.S., gifts were what the recipient needed. On my twenty-first birthday in April of my third year at Loyola, I vividly remember my Dad coming out to my porch (I had taken over my brother Pat's porch bedroom when he was married two years before). He had a small package in his hand, wrapped in brown paper. Inside was my birthday gift—a medium-sized office-style stapler with a box of refills. Half-serious, only half-laughing at himself, he said, "I think you're old enough to have one of your own."

I used that stapler until I got married seven years later, and one of its descendants is never far from where I am working. That gift epitomized my dad's attitude towards giving gifts and doing things for others—one gave others what they needed, with no relationship to the usual perception of what gifts are made of. I saw him do that for my mother when, her arm being broken one time, he found a claw-like grabber which gave her access to the top shelf of the cupboard without the necessity of mounting a ladder. He presented that to her as if he were giving her diamonds. Later on I know he applied his "what is needed" principle to the first gift he gave to the Poor Clares, a contemplative order following the rule of St. Francis (and his "sister-moon," St. Clare) which had a convent near his business on Laflin Ave. in Chicago. The sisters there devoted their lives to praising God and interceding for sinful and troubled mankind. Only certain "lay" sisters, who were entrusted with the care of the house, met the public. In the chapel was perpetual Eucharistic adoration and my father loved to stop on his way home from work to say some prayers.

Dad had observed one of these sisters lugging around a heavy wooden ladder as she cleaned and put up decorations for the liturgical feasts, and he saw a need. "Sister," he said to the diminutive nun, "I am going to buy you one of these lightweight aluminum ladders that have come out, and you can move it about much more easily."

"Oh, Mr. Grogan," she quickly responded, for she had come to know his name when he had asked for prayers and left donations in the past, "I don't need one of those, but we do sorely need several other things. They are . . . ."

Thus began my father's more-involved gifting of the Poor Clares, love for whom he and my mother passed on to us. At Christmastime, though, gifts were for fun and frivolity, so he always went shopping about three o'clock on Christmas Eve, entertaining the clerks at Bonwit Teller or Marshall Field's with prompts like "my wife is this tall and this wide—what can you give me for her?" One year he gave all the girls panties, and I still have the bright red bloomers that he bought. Often he would adorn himself with these, using the elastic at the waist to secure them on his forehead, at the Christmas Eve party.

His giving was a giving of joy. He told us children tales based on a semi-delinquent fictional character he had created named "Beevo Bosco Booze Kettle." He invested this character with adventures he would have like to have had. One centered around Beevo's imbibing some beer, so much, in fact, that in order for him to fit in the front door, his mother had to puncture his tummy in the way one punctures a balloon. To Beevo's alliterative name, he often added references to his backside as his "bondoonie"—a word that still lives in our family.

R.S.G. was a man whose gifts truly enriched and delighted both the giver and the receiver, and I think his attitude of savoring the fun of giving is with me today.

Recently a particularly vitriolic biography of Nancy Reagan was published, and one of the incidents in it told of her wrapping up for her grandson a teddy bear which she found lying around the house. It turned out that this was the boy's own teddy bear which he had left when visiting. It has often been known that I have gone to my "cedar chest" for gifts when an occasion arises, and while most of the gifts there have been purchased when I happened to come across them, there are a few, I admit, which I received and intend to pass along.

2 ~ Gifts in the RSG Tradition: Useful & Loving

My theory is that such a gift gives pleasure twice—to the first person who receives it and the one who is the later recipient. This tendency, however, inspired my cousin Betty Murphy to give me handkerchiefs with my name one year.

My father's habit of giving useful gifts continued into the early years of my marriage when, having himself found the house my husband and I were living in, he would drop in at least once a week, ostensibly to "use the plumbing," but actually to deliver a new broom or bucket or chamois for windows—all the things that new housedwellers need.

Not only did he give unorthodox gifts, but he enjoyed giving them in unusual ways. One time, the religious order which staffed the high school I had attended needed money for a mother house and permitted its members to visit homes of their friends "to beg" upon invitation of these same friends. So unusual was this chance to be able to entertain School Sisters of Notre Dame for dinner that I went to my mother, an accomplished cook and gracious entertainer, and asked her to host such a party. My beloved high school English teacher and writer, Sister Mary Hester Valentine, along with the much-admired principal of the Academy of Our Lady, arrived one Sunday and shared a roast beef dinner with all the trimmings with us. After dinner, my father excused himself from the table and said, "The Sisters and I have to retire to the living room so that I can see if their cause is worthy." Judging from the gales of laughter emitting from the living room, they didn't have to beg too abjectly to get the check which helped to make Mequon, later lost in the lean period of religious communities in the late '60s, a reality.

So today, whenever I think of an "off-beat" gift, I see my father proffering an aluminum ladder to the Poor Clare Nun, giving me a metal stapler in the early morning of my twenty-first birthday, or making the sisters "beg" for the check he was giving to their religious community. He has a puckish smile and a glow in those very blue eyes which say, "Giving should provide pleasure for the giver and receiver."

III
The St. Louis Connection and the Grandfather Who Was My "Pal"

St. Louis in the summer was a world of blistering heat where a box of chocolate candy brought by a visitor and left on the living room mantel one evening would be guarded by an army of ants marching all the way from the front door some twenty-five feet away to that mantel the next morning. It was also a place where, in the house run by my aunt who went off to Rubicam's daily, I was somewhat in the relaxed care of my grandfather, a retired Metropolitan Life insurance salesman. James Travers had been a good salesman in his day and often had won prizes for his monthly tally, a pitcher and glasses set or a pewter platter, according to my mother. But now he tended to enjoy his daily walks to the tavern a few blocks from my aunt's house, and I, of course, always went with him.

We had a "deal," he and I, that every time he had a beer, I was to have a coke, and he honored that bargain religiously. On Mondays they served hot roast beef sandwiches free for lunch to regular customers at Balducci's, his favorite local pub. We were always first in line to be served. One night I foolishly bragged that I had had seven cokes that day, and that brought my aunt's volatile wrath on my grandfather; from then on she tried to supervise my schedule more carefully. Swimming lessons at a nearby Y.W.C.A. were introduced, and one of my older high-school-age cousins, of whom there were many around St. Louis, was drafted to take me to them. One morning I was about to leave for my lesson when I realized that Grandpa had not come down for breakfast and I dashed up the stairs before leaving to say goodbye. There was my grandfather, fallen back on the bed in the act of putting on his socks, felled by a massive heart attack.

3 ~ The St. Louis Connection & The Grandfather Who Was My "Pal"

Though he was already dead, the priest was, of course, called, and many uncles, aunts, and cousins arrived just as he did. They gathered in the high-ceilinged second floor bedroom to offer the prayers for the dying, and one of my grown-up boy cousins, seeing my nine-year-old face at the door, closed it. "Didn't he know," I raged, "that this was my grandfather too, and that just yesterday we had made our daily pilgrimage to Balducci's together, over the hot St. Louis streets of 1939, joined in the secret closeness and unexpressed understanding which only the old and the young can have?" I never forgot the lesson learned there that children close to someone in life should never be excluded in death.

Evidently, this grandfather had been quite a colorful character in his youth before he settled down to work for the Metropolitan. At age eighteen, enraged by what my mother always said was the "condescension" of the British teachers who were sent over to "civilize" the Irish in their schools in the nineteenth century, he "hit" an English schoolmaster. The whole family had to leave Ireland. Then, to crown their sorrow, their mother died at sea. To the surprise of the people on board, the ship reversed course and returned to Queenstown, later called Cobh, where she was buried.

But then they came to St. Louis and I don't know what hardships the motherless Irish family might have suffered there. I know only that within some years my grandfather was in search of a young woman whom he remembered from Ireland to offer her marriage. The only barrier was that she had entered a convent in America which he then had to visit and persuade her to leave. Whether he used charm and persuasion or more devious tactics, I do not know, but persuade her he did. He and Elizabeth Shanley Travers had five children, of whom my mother was the fourth. My grandmother died in her early forties of pernicious anemia—unfortunately a catch-all phrase, much used at the time, leaving much unanswered.

But the debonair man in his seventies who had been my "pal," as he called himself (meanwhile gesturing as if to slit his throat), was my taste of that special relationship which comes between those whose battles have been already lost or won and those whose identity struggles haven't started yet. And when my grown-up cousin closed the door upon me at age nine, I secretly resolved never to deny a child who had laughed with and loved a person in life the chance of experiencing that person's death and grieving over it.

Years later that memory was to remind me not to exclude five-year-old Mary Kate and four-year-old Edmund when my own mother, their grandmother, died. She had taken care of them only a few weeks before she entered the hospital for the surgery from which she never recovered. The fact that they both remember her, unlike my father who died when Mary Kate was four weeks and Edmund not yet born, has given them at least an image to which to attach family stories.

My grandfather's death did not halt the trips to St. Louis. My brother and I were to remember what it was to have a wonderful extended family there to visit, just a train ride away, but sufficiently distant to have a romantic aura attached.

IV
HOW I DISCOVERED THE REAL WORLD: THE LOOP AND MARSHALL FIELD'S

Soon the '40s and World War II were to make a big change in everyone's life, not perhaps in the daily pattern but in what we thought and heard about. Where Franklin D. Roosevelt had been someone we heard speak once in a while in his fireside chats and whose pictures dominated the storefront Democratic headquarters (and whose wife Eleanor seemed to like to be away from him a lot), he was now the man who solemnly led us in war. Though later criticized for many of the pacts he made, it was generally acknowledged that he had been America's savior, in spite of what Father Coughlin said in his newspaper, *Social Justice*, hawked outside our parish church each Sunday by "outsiders who wanted to cause disruption," our pastor Monsignor Shewbridge warned us.

I remember, just as the '40s began, a trip to Maxwell Street to an open-air market which we visited one Sunday morning each winter to gaze and sniff at the smelly array of food, clothing, and other amenables sold in the stalls. It was made quite clear to us that we were there to look, not buy, and such sights as a large foot sticking out of a curtained stall accompanied by yells of its owner whose bunions were being removed further persuaded us of this attitude. One day, however, one of the Jewish merchants grabbed my father and brother as we passed, exhorting my father to "buy a new coat for this son of yours, because you ought to be ashamed at how short his sleeves are." It was true that my tall skinny brother had reached that adolescent growth spurt early and his clothes were not keeping pace. The merchant's remarks having been conveyed to my mother, she quickly scheduled a shopping trip to the Loop, whether it was the year for buying a jacket or not. Conservative spending habits were deeply ingrained in my mother and father and, though I think my mother would secretly have loved to go on a "fling" occasionally, she abided by the family tradition which was to pay cash and buy good quality when needed, not when an impulse dictated it.

The Loop was the Jerusalem of all shopping pilgrimages. While one might go to Frank's Department Store on 79th for shoes and to Wieboldt's and Sears Roebuck at 63rd & Halsted for new slacks and occasionally a sweater, downtown was where the "action" was. When I was ten years old, my father said that I was old enough to go down to the Loop alone, and though my mother might have had a few misgivings, she agreed that it was a good thing to "know how to get around." Our two-flat building, occupied by my father, mother, brother, and me on the second floor and my unmarried aunt and not-yet-married uncle on the first, was just a little over a block from the end of a streetcar line. There one could ride an hour on one car, go through a variety of Chicago neighborhoods, and finally reach Madison St. just two blocks from its intersection with State, which everyone knew was the busiest corner of the world.

So, off I went one summer day with a whole dollar saved from allowances and birthdays to be wisely spent downtown. Lunch was always a part of any such trip, but I knew my dollar wouldn't take me to Marshall Field's where Mother always took her St. Louis visitors. Upon debarking from the Clark Street car, which is what this streetcar was known as, I spied E.W. Rieck's Beanery. I had been there once or twice with my dad when he infrequently came downtown to do banking.

But I was hardly prepared for the scene that greeted me as I entered—strong coffee aromas mixed with the spicy savor of vegetable soup and baked beans, all of these served by men wearing white chefs' hats, harboring often toothless mouths and the general look of tough old sailors such as those I saw on the screen of the Capitol Theatre at 79th St. (It was one of those moving-starlight-ceilinged theatres which gave away free dishes on Monday nights and caused our street, three blocks away, to be crowded on Saturday nights with parked cars.)

I ordered both baked beans which we often had with ham at home and a cup of coffee which, though not encouraged, I was allowed there too. One of the fugitives from *Mutiny on the Bounty* behind the counter showed no surprise at a biggish ten-year old ordering such a thing, conveyed the order to his collaborator in the kitchen, and soon was sending down the counter, from the front of the restaurant, two covered containers which almost flew past me. A kind gentleman who looked like my father gathered that I didn't know the protocol, grabbed them as they were about to speed past, and anchored them firmly in place. They tasted heavenly.

I'm sure that day I walked through Marshall Field's and possibly bought a hair ribbon at Woolworth's or Kresge's, both of which were represented downtown. But I remember only the "old salt" who sent my "baked and a cup" down the counter and the scalding delicious vittles I guzzled on my foray into the world as an independent.

When I regaled them at dinner about my experience, my mother looked a little bit fearful, but my dad, Chicago-phile that he was, smiled in satisfaction that he had fathered another Loop-lover, oblivious to the fact that I might have been in any danger. And in that long ago, Arcadia-like world, I'm sure that danger was minimal, indeed.

V
Mother

I remember writing at least two essays in high school about my colorful father whose reputation was well known among my friends. Such things as passing out red rubber balls from Maxwell Street to my high-heeled "sophisticated" senior friends at an open house we had the Sunday after Easter did not go unreported even at the lady-like high school I attended. But my mother, soft of voice and sweet of temper, was the one who was always "there" for me—and for others who needed her.

Genevieve Travers Grogan with her lovely complexion and prematurely gray hair was a "beautiful woman," my friend and teacher Sister Hester told me. That was a shock to me at sixteen, but when she added that nobody can be considered truly beautiful until she is at least thirty-five, I knew she was using a standard of judgment that was not mine. More than forty years later, I have expanded my vision.

Oftentimes I would return home from Longwood to find one of my brother's college friends ensconced in the kitchen with a fresh warm slice of homemade bread and a cup of coffee. Or my own pal Alice Gerrity, who had forgotten her keys, would be hunkered down over the table ostensibly doing her homework but actually sharing some of her problems with Mom as Mom ironed her omnipresent load of linen tablecloths. When Alice's mother got home from "driving the Nuns to the depot," one of her "goodguy" acts, Alice would go home. Today, a teen-ager taking refuge in a neighbor's house would probably ask to switch on the television, but these young people were deep in conversation with my *MOTHER*. Imagine that! My brother and I discovered later that these confidences often concerned very personal decisions, things my brother and I would never hear—like the time Alice was almost "booted out" of nurses' training because of the visits of a young doctor to her nursing station. My mother heard these stories before I did, things that prompted John Mills, one of

Pat's friends, to say to me when my mother died, "She was your mother, but she was *my* friend."

Genevieve's nurturing instincts had been well honed in early-twentieth-century St. Louis when she and her older sister Mary had cared for their mother who had pernicious anemia. My mother believed that their Tuesday novenas kept her alive at least one extra year, but my grandmother died at forty-six when my mother was sixteen. Soon afterwards, my mother enrolled at Rubicam's Business College, the school made famous in Tennessee Williams's *Glass Menagerie* when Laura, the lame daughter, dropped out of her class when scolded by a strict teacher. Rubicam's was a proper place which prided itself on developing the perfect secretary and the consummate business woman. Mary and Genevieve Travers both later became teachers at Rubicam's. When a tradesman would default on a promised delivery, my mother would put on her Rubicam's roar, and quote Mr. Charles Rubicam: "Miss Travers, do not tell them the job will be done on Tuesday. Give yourself an extra day and you will be safe." Since the Rubicams ran a roofing company as well as a business college, they wanted the theories they taught to be applied as well.

My mother married and came to Chicago at twenty-seven, abandoning her business career, but she was always able to manage dinner parties, and her diplomatic powers took some of their strength from that early period too. One Saturday I returned home from a day of work at the Newberry Library, the edifice which was later to provide me with my husband, Ed. Father Stratman, my graduate school advisor, was ensconced in the living room with an old-fashioned in his hand and the Saturday opera music on the radio, while my mother drifted back and forth from the kitchen keeping him "informed." She said Father Stratman, a far-North Sider, had been "in the neighborhood" visiting a sick friend of his mother and had wanted to say "hello" to my mother whom he had met at a Loyola function. Father Stratman never forgot those lamb chops we all ate, and a year later when I thought that all hope of getting my master's degree in June was lost because of the late submission of readers' copies of my thesis, Father Stratman approached each reader with a request for haste. I'm sure he thought less of the *Duchess of Malfi*, the thesis subject, than he did of my mother's flower-decked table, my father's warmth, and—oh yes—those broiled lamb chops.

When my mother died in 1965, four of our five children had been born, but I prayed for another. Robert, named for my father, was the answer, and I can't help thinking that she asked God to send Rob as a reminder of my father's benevolent good humor. They were a great pair—Genevieve and Rob Grogan—and we are still enjoying their influence.

VI
THE NEIGHBORHOOD—
OUR LOST AMERICA

As I recall my happy childhood on Green Street, I know that, like many another's early years, it was full of self-doubts, insecurities, loving friendships, and great dreams which youngsters all over the world share. But ours had a certain ambience which all of us who lived in slightly different ways in that somewhat sheltered pocket of the South Side of Chicago shared. Some of the most vivid memories have to do with the sounds of Green Street. There was Mrs. Demling, our next-door neighbor, quick of foot in her thrice-daily trips to the Granitine garbage box at the alley. The click of her heels, borne through the open windows of our second-floor flat, often told us that Mrs. Demling had finished her house-cleaning, planned her dinner, and was off to the Capitol Theatre, one of the few places where one was sure to be cool for the afternoon. And the car which enabled her to make a quick getaway served all us neighborhood kids very well too, for often she was there at St. Leo School on rainy days to give us all a ride home for the all-too-short lunch period. Since Jean Demling, the youngest of the three Demling children, was a year older than my brother Pat and five years ahead of me, those trips would presumably stop when Jean went on to high school at Longwood, but that was not the case. Inexplicably, Mrs. Demling turned up quite often at just the right moment.

Perhaps the force of old habits made Mrs. Demling turn her car that way, but more likely she felt the bond of neighbors who shared births and First Communions and nine-year-old girls' birthday parties to which the guest of honor had invited forty classmates, much to her mother's chagrin, but not to her neighbors' surprise. On the day of the party there were five cakes delivered by neighbors to our back door, neighbors whose children were beyond that stage but who remembered those days well.

Mrs. Demling, of the lifts to school, paid dearly for her wisps of freedom later, when poor Mr. Demling, suffering from hardening of the arteries, paced the gangway between our homes, soliloquizing about the money he had lost in the crash of 1929. We heard the stockbrokers called diverse names and, as children, wondered why he lamented since his three children went to Notre Dame and St. Mary's College variously, emerging as a fire department official and two teachers, sponsored by "Uncle Pete." What we didn't fully appreciate was his deeply layered sorrow at not being able to send them to college himself, as he had planned.

Another sound that became familiar was the footsteps of Mr. Wortel, our butter and egg man. First, brother Raymond and later, when he went to war, Mr. Wortel brought butter and eggs straight from the country. No sneakers in those days, they climbed the wooden steps in heavy leather-soled shoes, clumping their way and gaining my father's appellation, "Forty Horsemen."

Mr. Wortel regaled, once, my wide-open childish ears with an exciting account of how he would go into his almost-dark basement, light a candle, and examine every egg, the candle glow enabling him to see if an embryonic chicken was within. We thought it sounded like Halloween and imagined our loud-footed egg man descending into the candle-lit cavern to perform his magic. As time went on, Mr. Wortel stopped bringing butter to his increasingly diet-conscious customers, but the tradition continued, for my mother had him deliver eggs to us, the young folks. At last sighting, Mr. Wortel at eighty-plus was still delivering eggs, to the children of the children of his original customers.

These neighborly sounds, along with the bell of the knife sharpener, the call of the "Rag Man" who went down our alley singing "Rags, Old Iron," and the erratic barking habits of my brother's wayward dog were the sounds of Green Street which bring back the poignant memories of the people who occasioned them. This was the era of streetcars on trolleys over on Halsted Street and horseshoe games on Sunday in the vacant lot next to the trolley turn-around. It was the time of hot tamales from the man with the cart on 78th Street and girls' professional softball games at Shewbridge Field a couple of miles away, named for our pastor at St. Leo's.

6~ The Neighborhood—Our Lost America

We never knew that we had a closed society, but when my grade school class had a twenty-fifth reunion and invited everyone back, a Croatian girl, who had worn babushkas up to her forehead and whose shoes were pointed, responded, "Not on your life!" Our society had not yet discovered the advantages of multi-culturalism, and evidently we were very insular. Aside from the Italian shoemaker, the Jewish lady who ran the paper stand, and the Chinese laundryman, the whole world was white, and of Irish or German descent, and, of course, Catholic, with just a few Lutherans or Methodists to provide contrast.

When I say insular, that isn't quite an accurate description. We took the Clark Street car downtown from its origin at 81st and Halsted, and we never thought of ourselves as other than part of the great metropolis. Whenever we went downtown, my brother of the delicate stomach was sure to get sick right in Chinatown, so I became a regular window-shopper at the exotic display windows. Mrs. Gleason, my friend Marion's mother, taught school at Maxwell and Halsted, and we begged to correct her spelling papers. My father's company, at 49th and Rockwell, had places nearby where one could get sleeves lengthened (a family need) much more reasonably than 79th and Halsted, and we knew there were equally exciting spots to discover once we were released from the constraints of a geographical neighborhood. Why, after all, there were not only the streetcars and buses, but "L's" which went anywhere—anywhere a Chicago child of the '30s or '40s wanted, anyway!

VII
More Neighborhood Vignettes: Faith and Hope Transplanted

Our home at 81st and Green was in the center of a thriving, second-generation Irish and German neighborhood, with the preponderance being Irish. But these were not people who looked nostalgically back at their native land, wishing they could be there. No, that was an emotion which, if it struck at all, was one saved for their children and a time when air travel had become easier and cheaper. These folks were here to stay as, in many cases, their parents had been. They, along with many other immigrants, planned to make their mark here. There was no romanticizing of green hills and soft brogues. Though they had found the streets were not paved in gold, they were here. For immigrants who already knew the language and were literate, it was a far more attractive place to be than the rocky terrain of County Mayo. I never heard a single story of their encountering signs which read "No Irish need apply." They got jobs, worked hard, and never looked back.

Whether my Grogan grandparents had had any desire to return I do not know, and I think my Aunt Bessie Grogan, oldest surviving member of the family, would have told me about it if there had been any. She was the one who knew how to contact the family in Ireland when Betty and I were planning our trip in 1953, and it was she who wrote James Padden, my cousin, the wonderful "thirty-seven-year-old bachelor unless one of the fair sex takes pity on me." James took Betty and me all over in his Ford Anglia. The fair sex did, of course, some years later in the person of Agnes, a lovely nurse whom we met in 1967 when we were there for Ed's sabbatical with Mary Kate, Edmund, and John. Certainly my maternal grandfather, forced to leave at eighteen after his encounter with the English schoolmaster, never spoke of a return. His success as a Metropolitan salesman in St. Louis made it a far more attractive place to be.

7 ~ More Neighborhood Vignettes: Faith & Hope Transplanted

At 79th Street or nearby, we had almost everything we needed. In the 1920s post-war era, huge edifices were erected as banks; ours was the Mutual National, and Pat and I were encouraged to open savings accounts at an early age there. The Auburn Park branch library was just across the street, and I remember being very disappointed one summer day when they refused to let me return the books I had taken out in the morning and had already finished. They said you couldn't have the same date stamped for withdrawal and return. At age ten, that seemed to me the height of stupidity.

There was a four-floor department store, Frank's, at the corner of 79th and Green, quite a plus for a small neighborhood shopping spot. Mr. Frank, a small friendly-to-customers man, walked up and down the aisles, probably we thought to check on employees because we heard that the wages they paid neighborhood ladies were penurious. Later on, when one of my grade school classmates, Pat O'Donnell, worked at the candy counter after school, that was confirmed.

But they had a wonderful shoe department, staffed by sober-faced balding men who measured your feet and pinched toes and even looked through the fluoroscope machine they had, to see how close your toes were to the end.

Some years later, the Gudauskas family who had bought the Foxes' house next door tried to buy shoes there and, according to the wonderfully expressive Mrs. Gudauskas, could find nothing. They are all made for "you Irish people with narrow feet," she complained, "not for the Eastern European peasant." She may have had a peasant's feet, but she had an aristocrat's soul, and we listened to her music spilling out through the open French windows next door, enthralled. Her husband, my father's doctor, was equally interesting, and when he visited my father, he often found his way to the porch-bedroom which I occupied, usually strewn with papers. Once when he did that, it was particularly messy, and my mother tried to apologize. He stopped her, saying, "The professor must have papers all around." The Gudauskas family left for California soon after my father's death in 1960, and, sadly, we never heard from them again. It's a theory of mine that this is what happens to people who move to California—a theory supported by all kinds of evidence, albeit anecdotal.

There was no sort of neighborhood organization in those days. Who needed it when one had the parish and the local schools, both Catholic and public, which were focal points. The Protestant children, next door, the Foxes and the Glinkes, went to Gresham, and Mrs. Phillips, two doors away, drove her children there too. George, her son, had a heart condition and needed extra care. When the war came in 1941, all the neighborhoods were organized into block clubs for civilian defense purposes, and much was made of electing block captains and having meetings to prepare for all the eventualities which we prayed would not happen. Aunt Bessie returned from one of these meetings with a story about the Paisleys. Mr. Paisley, a tall articulate business executive, was our block captain, and at the meeting, Mrs. Paisley, a very short woman, ventured an opinion. Mr. Gavin, an Irishman "from the old sod," as they termed it, did not like what she said and expressed it thus: "Will that little girl please consider some other factors in our plan?"

Mr. Paisley, realizing that his spirited little wife would not like the form of reference, replied, "That little girl, sir, is my wife!" Later, the now-widow Mrs. Paisley, who was a Trinity College graduate, took a teaching job at Visitation High School. Returning from early Mass one day, I remember being startled to attention by her greeting as she walked to the bus, "Good morning, Mary Sunshine. What new and untried adventures await you today?"

Years later, while standing on an "L" platform in Evanston, I spotted the diminutive form of Mrs. Paisley. We had a wonderful conversation about the frequent trips she took her grandchildren on while living in a retirement home near her daughter. Hers was one of the blithe spirits undaunted by the years.

Presiding over our entire neighborhood was the lofty dome of the Capitol Theater which got double features of the latest movies. Next door was a little restaurant which we repaired to when the show was over and which became the gathering place of young people after late Mass on Sunday.

In essence, we were a tightly knit community before the term became popular, bound by ties of culture and faith and the conviction that the world would be good to us out there if we just worked hard and employed the twin virtues of thrift and honesty. It was an era of optimism and hope.

VIII
Diamond Lake—
My Childhood Garden of Eden

As I look back over my childhood of the '30s and '40s, I see the patterns emerge as comforting and familiar: the six-block walk back to St. Leo's School after lunch—and a pain in the pit of your stomach if you had eaten too much; the time in January of 1940 when the temperature was 18 below zero and after my brother and I, enveloped in scarves, had walked to school, the nuns sent us all home, clucking "your mothers should have had more sense." There were Sunday mid-day dinners, one time at our flat and the next week at Aunt Bessie's downstairs. As my father carved the obligatory roast beef, we had the four-ounce glasses which had come with Kraft cheese spread, now full of beer, because Dad said we had to "keep Uncle Jimmy working." Uncle Jim, who looked much like my father, worked for the Keeley Brewery. One Sunday, my Uncle Joe Grogan, a bachelor until he was forty who lived with his older sister Bessie downstairs, shot a rubber band at the cuckoo as it came out of the clock brought to her from Germany, and we never saw the bird again. In the main, Sundays were a time to let down the guard and relax as a family.

But these were ordinary things, we thought, and others were "special," such as trips to St. Louis and Diamond Lake. That was where we rented a cottage for two weeks each summer in August from a Czech lady, Mrs. Zuschlag, who had lived next door to my parents during the first year of their marriage, at the end of which my brother Pat was born. Mr. Z's German carpenter nephews had built a two-story frame cottage on an island in the middle of this large stone-bottomed lake near Cassopolis, Michigan, and Mrs. Z and her husband, childless, began taking Pat up there for a few days in the early 1930s. Soon we were renting the cottage for two weeks each summer with a variety of relatives and close family associates. Betty, my cousin from St. Louis who regularly spent summers with us, was soon able to drive the car my Grandfather Travers had provided, and she was our lifeguard and life-line to town for my non-driving mother. Dad, who could hardly let Chicago Granitine take care of itself during those struggling years, came up only on Sundays, driving back early Monday morning. I can still see him waiting at the boat dock when we were ferried across on Sunday a.m, straw-hatted and clad in a ridiculous sweater, ready to drive us to Cassopolis for Mass, and swallowing his city boy's distaste for bucolic inconvenience. It was real inconvenience at Diamond Lake with no electricity for the early years and no plumbing ever. We pumped our water for drinking and cooking, took our baths in the lake, and cheerfully used the outhouse behind the cottage just this side of the woods.

A wonderful woman who had worked for our family when my mother had been sick one time, Mrs. Doran, came along to help her each summer, and sometimes one of my Travers cousins from St. Louis was invited to join us. A great deal of effort and devotion was put into this vacation each year by my mother whose orange juice squeezer was attached to a tree outside the cabin door and my father who had to "woo" Mrs. Zuschlag each season to rent us the cottage which had represented so much effort on the part of her family. A fifty-pound chunk of ice had to be purchased and lugged from the ferry dock every three days, to keep our food from spoiling, and Mrs. Doran and my mother prepared meals on an ancient kerosene stove which looked as though it had come from the Black Forest a hundred years previously. But nothing was too much trouble, they all said, to help provide this yearly two weeks on an island where we swam, often three times a day, blistered our hands with the oars of the rowboat, and played endless rummy at night often by the light of the kerosene lamp.

This sturdy fortress-like "cottage" had an ancient wind-up phonograph, and one record played constantly, "Oh, I Married a Belle of Barcelona." The outhouse had two holes and a lock on the outside so that small animals would not get in. My brother with Dick and Jerry Travers would wait sometimes until someone like me had gone in and then turn the outside bolt. The person would not be confined long, for with so many people living in the cottage he would soon be rescued. If my mother or Mrs. Doran was the one stuck, we would feel their wrath in our tummies, for dinner would be late and our rummy games for the night delayed.

Diamond Lake, to all who shared even part of one of the weeks, represented, at least for the children, the halcyon existence we thought might have prevailed once in that Garden given to Adam and Eve. We laughed and argued over cards each night, lighted everyone's way to the outhouse before bedtime, and read our books by flashlight after the grown-ups, who worked much harder than we did, had gone to sleep. Only a slight tightening of my mother's jaw reminded us on the final day that this had not gone without price. The cottage had to be cleaned to the highest standards. Unless we left the place as Mrs. Zuschlag had given it to us, Mother warned, she might never rent to us again. That was beyond imagination so we all pitched in. Diamond Lake was part of the family history for another year.

IX
AUNT BESSIE AND UNCLE JOE

My childhood and youth were full of characters who, while not quite out of Charles Dickens, were far more interesting than I dreamed at the time. Aside from my father who was a stern businessman on the one hand and delightful comedian on the other, there were Aunt Bessie and Uncle Joe downstairs.

Bessie was a born greeter, and that was the job she held at the Packard Motor Car Company—switchboard operator. Her fabled popularity there stemmed from her pert responses to questions from callers and bosses and her amazing ability to remember phone numbers for all the executives, whose calls had to be made through her board. She had to remember their phone numbers, the numbers of their regular clients whom they called often, as well as the railroads, and, later, travel agents. Evidently, Bessie did it well, because at Christmastime she usually had to be sent home in a luxurious Packard with her horde of gifts.

Starting off as a telephone operator, Bessie found her way to Packard early. Those were the days when children went to work after grade school, the early 1900s. Family lore had it that when she was sixteen and working nights for the telephone company, she would bring her streetcar transfer home for my father to use in order to get to business college.

Bessie was the 1900s version of the independent woman, but one who took family responsibility seriously. My grandmother, who had been such a dominant figure in her prime that it was said she had supervised every move of the workmen building the Grogan house on 51st Street, had suffered greatly when her oldest son John died at seventeen, reputedly of pneumonia. Grandma was never the same again, my uncle said, and so Bessie and Lucy, the next-oldest girl, took over the running of the house.

Bessie, now the oldest and far more assertive than gentle, convent-bred Lucy, who would die in 1925 before my parents' marriage, sought the job at Packard to escape from night work. She told the story of applying to Packard, getting the job, and going into a restaurant nearby to have a celebratory pie and coffee. Only when she was almost finished did she realize that she did not have sufficient money to pay. She waited until a prosperous, gray-haired man advanced to the cashier, then cut ahead of him, plunking her bill down and saying airily, "The man behind will pay!"

I don't know if Bessie ever came close to marriage, but she told me one time of how a man, who had taken her out to dinner in her thirties, gazed in the moonlight at her prematurely white hair and pronounced her the most beautiful blond he had ever seen. I suspect that Bessie saw family responsibility as her not wholly unwelcome lot, and so she joined that number of aunts, coming to maturity in the early 1920s after World War I, who remained single.

When the stock market crash came in 1929 and people who had driven luxury Packard sedans were jumping out of windows or seeking solace in sanitariums, Bessie was told that she could either give up her job or take a salary cut of almost half. She chose the latter.

She was always to me just "Aunt Bessie," who occupied the first floor of our comfortable two-flat on Green Street and was the source of numerous beneficences to my brother Pat and me, including at least one vacation. She brought interesting ladies home, like the voluble Catherine Ginocchio, the charming Mary Gallagher, and the deep-voiced Margaret Cullen, who enriched our lives. Her later years were clouded by severe diabetes, which some members of the family thought was brought on by the death of my first cousin, Bill Grogan, at eighteen in the Navy from a blood disease he had contracted in the service.

My father always provided her the security of her own apartment in our building and, to the end, she insisted on walking to 81st and Halsted each night just before ten to get an evening paper. That was their generation's version of turning on the ten o'clock news. Bessie died suddenly in January 1960 when we were expecting our first child. One Sunday night a month later, my husband and I were playing cards with my mother and dad at Green Street when we heard

9 — Aunt Bessie & Uncle Joe

the outside vestibule door close at just about that time. With hardly a pause, my dad looked up playfully and remarked with a shake of his head, "Bessie!" That was the Grogans' way of relieving the tension when situations might arouse an undue show of sentiment. Like many Irish, they chose to defuse any potential over-emotion, a habit which is the background for the Irish wake, often described as full of both laughter and tears.

Another person who is a vivid "character" from my childhood was my Uncle Joe Grogan, youngest in my father's family and a bachelor until he was forty. He lived downstairs at Green Street in the flat which Bessie maintained, along with her and their wonderful older-lady housekeeper, Mrs. Gordon.

Joe was a "late bloomer." While I never knew exactly why Joe was "different" from the other Grogans, I suspected he had had a "wild youth," which probably meant that he had stayed out late and not found a steady job right after school. Joe's eyesight had suffered from a case of measles he had had as a boy, and he had left school early, not learning his barbering until later. But in spite of heavy glasses, Joe was an avid reader, and he often told us of articles whose subjects my parents never would have mentioned.

My brother Pat and I saw him as a less authoritative version of our parents' generation who stayed with us when they had to attend a wake. We enjoyed his iconoclastic view of the world. On Sundays, we alternated dinner sites, eating at Aunt Bessie's one Sunday and our apartment upstairs the next. One Sunday, my father, who repressed his puckishness during the week as president of Chicago Granitine, joined his brother Joe in an escapade which certainly must have angered Aunt Bessie, but which Pat and I saw as high comedy. Bessie had a cuckoo clock, brought by a traveling relative of the Zuschlags from the Black Forest, and the annoying bird punctuated our Sunday dinners with his bawdy cries. One Sunday, my father and Joe made a "devil's pact," and when the nefarious bird emerged from his house for a salute, each shot a rubber band at him, stilling his raucous screech forever.

Another time, when my mother and Bessie were entertaining a group of ladies in our living room, Joe entered, took the typewriter out of my father's desk drawer, and amid a hushed living room, typed a letter in silence, disappearing back to the downstairs apartment without ever acknowledging the existence of the women. When my brother and I heard the account of this the next day, we imagined the pantomime and admired our suave uncle who was able to halt the din which we thought to be inseparable from social gatherings of women.

Joe furthered his career monetarily during World War II by cutting sailors' hair at a converted vocational school and prompting my father to pronounce that Joe's technique was totally ruined. He married Keltah Hopewell at age 40, and they had Roger, who became our youngest Grogan first cousin. I remember Joe's remarking in his sardonic way when Pat and I served as Roger's godparents at St. Rita's Church that we should go around and show the wedding couple at the front door the almost sure results of their commitment. After my father's death in 1960, I remember how Joe would suddenly appear on Wednesdays, barbers' day off, to drive my mother to our house where Mary Kate was a new baby.

Sadly, Joe did not see his son Roger reach manhood. He died in 1967 only two years after my mother. His satiric side had lost its Juvenalian edge, and he had become a much-loved symbol of happy days at Green Street.

X
Catherine and Others

As we call past images to our memories, some vivid characters emerge. Mine were not quite like Fagin from Charles Dickens or Jean Brodie who was "in her prime," but they gave color to my childhood. There was sweet and funny Mary Gallagher who was still around in her late seventies and able to put things in perspective for me when she wrote on my reaching that milestone, "Oh to be forty again!"

There was Catherine Ginocchio, brought to the family by Aunt Bessie. A second-generation Italian woman, she was short and stocky with a wonderful deep voice and laugh which the Grogans in their irreverence called a "whisky voice." Catherine lived in Oak Park with her combination of immediate family and cousins. They had combined one time when her young aunt was ill and needed Mrs. Ginocchio's help and never lived apart again. Catherine's brothers owned a wholesale fruit and vegetable business, Ginocchio Brothers, whose trucks I occasionally still see in the downtown area.

But Catherine was not the entrepreneur, building a business concern; she was the person for whom the phrase "generous to a fault" was coined. Whenever she came to Green Street, she carried shopping bags full of "Stop and Shop" goodies and banquet rolls from the Bismarck Hotel, the only place, she said, where one could procure those oval, crisp-crusted rolls, the type sitting on the plates with pats of real butter at the never-ending series of dinners given regularly for politicians at the Morrison or the Palmer House or the Stevens Hotel in downtown Chicago.

Catherine worked at some job procured for her by Marty Durkin, the only politically connected family friend to come out of the old neighborhood. Martin Durkin, head of the pipefitters union, had a short-lived term as Secretary of Labor in the Eisenhower administration where he was the token Democrat. In her office, Catherine's frequent trips to St. Peter's, the Franciscan Church in the Loop where everybody went to be "shriven" or to catch a Holy Day Mass, were observed by the cold and abrupt woman who was her superior. When this lady lost a very important set of keys one day, she asked Catherine to say a prayer to St. Anthony whom she had heard Catholics ask for help in finding lost items. Catherine agreed, but added that a donation for St. Anthony's poor would be exacted if the keys were found.

Sure enough, the missing keys were located and Catherine, on her way to St. Peter's, stopped by the woman's desk the next day. Obviously this person was not accustomed to thanksgiving for divine intervention, but she dug into her purse and, as she did, was reminded of her arthritic condition. Her remark, upon giving the five dollars to Catherine to donate, was, "This is for my shoulder too." This has been quoted in our family ever afterwards when someone was big on asking but short on appreciation.

Catherine never became wealthy because she did things like going to Marshall Field's each Christmas and asking the bookseller to choose just the right books for my brother Pat's and my children. How many other friends' grandchildren she did that for, I have no idea, but our daughter Mary Kate, an early and avid reader, remembers *The Little Princess*, sent in one of Catherine's Christmas boxes, as one of the great experiences of her childhood.

Other dramatic friends of Bessie's dotted the landscape of my youth. There was Margaret Cullen, tall and forbidding-looking when I was a child. She was the lady "who looks right through you," I told my mother. Margaret, an avid student of Spanish, "took her burial money" one year and went to Guatemala. As a teenager, I was mightily impressed by what I considered a valorous act.

My mother's distant cousins, the Maneys, rediscovered when she married my father and moved from St. Louis to Chicago, were not "ordinary" relatives. Three of these four ladies lived in the area and because one, Eleanor, had lost her husband and their mother, an invalid for years, had also recently died, my mother began inviting them for Christmas dinner in the early '40s. Having taken Eleanor's Packard, driven only on ceremonial occasions, out of the garage for the day, they would arrive laden with yuletide gifts. They always left plenty of time, but did not want to arrive unfashionably early, so

Angela once came into the hall, ringing the bell and announcing, "I know that we're much too early to come in, so we'll just wait out here in the car until it's time." R.S.G. later said only mother's certain disapproval prevented his saying, "O.K., we'll call you when it's time." Our family always has had the motto, "If it's funny, say it," but even by our loose criteria, he knew that would be going too far. But it would have been funny! The gifts they brought were inevitably large crystal or silver serving dishes, and I overhead my charitable mother saying one time almost to herself, "I don't have any more beds to store these under."

But store them she did, and we enjoyed the camaraderie of Eleanor, the very proper lady who, in her widowhood, went to work for the Internal Revenue Service, the red-haired Angela, a Chicago Public School teacher who intrigued her students with dramatic pronouncements that illuminated fourth-grade drudgery, and Zita, who was a musician as well as a teacher and gave us some "class." My father would say young people growing up without colorful people in their lives miss a lot. The Maney cousins were such memorable characters. One night after sharing some family event, they offered a ride to the western suburbs to Maxwell Green, my father's bachelor insurance man, also an occasional dinner guest. As they dropped him off at his designated corner, red-haired Angela said, "Goodnight, Mr. Brown." Zita added, "So long, Mr. Smith," and Eleanor, the driver, finished off with "Good-bye, Mr. Jones." As he closed the door and took off down the street at a good pace, my father's friend pronounced, "The name, ladies, is Green."

Though children and young adults were necessary helpers and conversational aides in my mother's maidless household, we were also called upon to be assistant hosts. Maxwell Green, who had known my father only as business executive, remarked to my dad one time after one of these dinners, "Mr. Grogan, your children do not seem much in awe of you."

Who could, with a man who passed out red rubber balls to high school seniors wearing heels and hats, who gave collapsing forks to people who ate on my mother's snowy tablecloth, and who had a name like "balloon head" or "five o'clock shadow" which he assigned to each one of my dates who performed the obligatory ritual of sitting in the living room and conversing with him while I got ready?

Of all the characters, he was, of course, the best because he did it all with a loving twinkle and a sympathy which enabled him to stop a joke or jibe just before it became outrageous—most of the time!

XI
Family Memories

January, 1940—almost ten years old. Fourth grade—my grandmother died. She was not someone who was a force in my life, rather a set memory. But she became more of a person when I heard that, years before, when the Grogans had been building their house in the French Church parish, she had come every day, positioning herself outside their future home. She said nothing—until the builders did something wrong! Then she directed and did so forcefully.

At that time the family consisted of her husband, Stephen, the quiet fireman for the railroad; John, the oldest; Bessie, the aunt of my childhood who lived downstairs and even included me sometimes in her vacation; Lucy, the only one of the Grogans who went to the Catholic school; my father, Rob; then Jim, eighteen months younger; and, finally, Joe, my bachelor-uncle until forty, who lived downstairs with my Aunt Bessie. Joe, who was many years younger than the oldest in the family, had weak eyes (from measles, we thought).

John died when he was very young—about seventeen, I think, and according to Uncle Jimmy, Grandma Grogan was never the same afterwards. I remember visiting her at Techny in the late '30s. I can see her sitting in a rocker in a sun room. We often took the long drive on Sunday to visit her in that faraway suburb, distant by 1930s standards. My dad, always ready to lighten the atmosphere, had brought my grandmother some spending money. He had a sheet of one-dollar bills, folded over. There were twenty ends that way, actually ten dollars. "Here they are, Mom," he said, "twenty bucks." With a rueful smile, she responded, "Ten, Rob, thanks."

I never remember any other comment of my grandmother. When she died, in one of the coldest Januaries ever, Bessie and Uncle Jim's wife, Kathryn, were out there, at Techny, with her. The midnight train stopped only on signal. Aunt Kathryn had a dramatic flair and realized that they should get back to Chicago to make funeral arrangements. So she asked one of the sisters for an old rag with which to signal. Sister gave her a suit of red flannel underwear and they made a flag, going out on the train tracks next to the station in the middle of the night.

My father, ultimately the most successful, had been the child in the family who had given his mother the most trouble. Sickly at birth, a doctor had suggested to Bridget Padden Grogan that she might never raise this child. A neighbor woman had suggested beer and he was given some of that daily, whether mixed with milk or alone, I do not know. Anyway, by the time he was in school, my dad was strong enough to cause mischief and he did. One teacher was quoted by my Aunt Bessie as saying, "It's too bad that the smartest boy in the class can't behave himself." Offered a penny to scrub the kitchen floor with his brother Jim, eighteen months younger, he gladly yielded the penny to Jim. Asked to get holy water at the church on Holy Saturday, Rob dipped into the family's new flush toilet which was full of nice clean water.

Given those beginnings, one might have expected a delinquent, but those were evidently youthful pranks or outlets which my father neatly sidelined to his social life when he took on work at Chicago Granitine. On St. Patrick's Day 1911, he was ready to tend to business. He no longer had to wait for older sister Bessie to come home from night work at the telephone company as he had done when attending business college. Then he used her streetcar transfer. Now he could afford his own carfare. St. Patrick's Day had ever been a day of prayer-ful and drink-full celebration for American Irish, so my father said a prayer to St. Patrick, wore a green tie, and advanced to his first and last job interview, with the Bohemian man, Mr. Washic, who was part of the family that owned Granitine. Robert Grogan got the job and became president ten years later when, sadly, Mr. Washic died of blood poisoning from a rusty nail encountered at work.

The work ethic of some Irish Americans bordered on the fanatical. I have since wondered if they had heard so many stories of signs on construction sites, "No Irish need apply," that they had to over-compensate. But I know that, in my childhood, being on time, paying one's debts if one had the bad judgment to incur them, and keeping one's word were all important. My mother told stories of her employer in St. Louis, the head of Rubicam's Roofing Company, cautioning her, "Miss Travers, do not say that we will have that job finished unless you are sure. Say we will *try*."

Being dependable and conscientious included paying for a music lesson one had to cancel or remunerating a workman you had to disappoint. It was all part of keeping your word, and both my mother's and father's families did that. It meant showing appreciation to people who had aided you when you needed them. Thus, each year when we went to Diamond Lake for a two-week cottage rental from Mrs. Zuschlag, we asked Mrs. Doran and one of her grandchildren to accompany us. Mrs. Doran was the large-boned woman whom my father hired in 1935 when my mother was recovering from a terrible infection which she got from the same germ—strep—that had given me scarlet fever the preceding winter. My father ran an ad, interviewed several women who answered it, and hired immediately the jolly lady who had lived through hard times raising her own three daughters and still in her sixties needed to do domestic work to make ends meet. She was an important person in our childhood, and being good to her was our job as much as our parents'.

The third-generation Irish-American childhood we experienced was a frugal one. But there was always enough to provide a plate for the person who mounted the wooden back steps and asked for it. Money which we were given in a weekly allowance was to spend, share, and save. If there was a division among those three purposes, it should go in favor of sharing, we were told.

We did not dream that we lived in a comfortable, ethno-centered world. Didn't everyone?

XII
Adolescent Uncertainties: Finding and Using One's Strengths

When I was eleven years old, a new and exciting activity surfaced in our little enclave of South Side Chicago, where the Clark Street car came to its final resting place or started on its run, depending upon where you came from and wanted to go. A lady was offering music lessons! She was a relative of the people who lived in the big corner two-flat at 82nd Street, and they spread the word that she would be coming in weekly from Indiana and giving piano lessons to local children, either alone or in a group.

I and my pals, Alice and Marion, wanted to learn to play. We sold the idea to our conservative second-generation Irish-American parents, who were willing to sponsor us, and we met to go next Saturday morning. The building had only a prairie of weeds between it and the streetcar line on Halsted Street which led to exotic places like Sears Roebuck and Wieboldt's at 63rd Street. There, we rang the downstairs bell, each identifying ourselves and, eagerly, we began our lessons, each buying a book and supposedly practicing daily. We had dreams that we should play like Paderewski, president of Poland and great composer who had come to world fame through a movie we had seen.

My Aunt Bessie, who lived in the apartment below us in this neighborhood of prosperous 1926-built brick two-flats, had an upright piano that would be available for my practice every afternoon. We bought our books, brought our two dollars each to Mrs. Scanlon, and began our musical courses. I did my scales and practiced my pieces, carefully using the key we kept for Aunt Bessie's apartment and confronting the piano every day. What came forth was shockingly unmelodic due partially to the untuned piano but in much larger measure to my lack of aptitude. My aunt, who worked at 26th and Michigan in "Automobile Row" as a switchboard operator of Packard Motor Car Company, had an older lady living with her. This woman, Mrs. Gordon (Gordie), who was grandmother-like to my brother and me, served as housekeeper all during the lean days of the Depression for almost no salary and became as close to being a member of our family as possible. Indeed, when she returned to us one summer years later after spending her "family" vacation in Toronto, she told us that she would not be going to them when she became more feeble, but hopefully would be able to stay with us, her family. We accepted that, and my mother took care of her through an amputation and finally to her death. But at the time of my musical escapade, she would be fixing dinner in the kitchen in anticipation of Bessie's return home. She wisely kept her comments to herself about the strange sound she heard from the living room.

One day, my mother came downstairs to give me a little encouragement. I was dumbfounded by the fact that she sat down and played "Believe Me If All Those Enduring Young Charms" right off, since I had never known her to have a lesson. It seemed not to encourage me, but to show me that my efforts, though diligent, were bearing no fruit. I kept that dirty little secret to myself, however, and went to music lessons each week, with chin up, staunchly denying the fact that I was stumbling in this simple process. Probably as motivation for me to "shape up," Mrs. Scanlon announced that Alice, Marion, and I, the three G's (as we were called because all of our last names began with the same letter), would play a trio at her next recital, to be given in a large room and to which parents would be invited.

I totally despaired. I had asked for the lessons; I had pleaded with my parents to let me do this. Now, I was going to have to suffer the consequences.

I knew better than to go to my father who could be rather brusque when he thought you might have been throwing away his hard-earned money, salary for his two-night and six-day weeks at Chicago Granitine. No, I went to my mother, gentle and seemingly vulnerable, having suffered a nervous breakdown some years before after a terrible siege of blood poisoning in her finger which resulted in a deformed right hand. I poured out my heart and was entirely shocked by her reaction. She started to laugh but checked herself as she enfolded my tearful figure, and sat down with me in the kitchen. We had a cup of coffee together and a piece of her homemade bread, eaten warm out of the oven against all dietary pronouncements. I had started to drink coffee that year, and unfortunately, my coffee-drinking ways coincided with the rationing of the same liquid in World War II. At eleven and twelve, I was not eligible for the coffee coupons that my mother and father received. Tea was in good supply since there was sufficient tea in the basement cabinet, kept, my father always said, "for scarce times." But we had a regular crusade to get to the store before the "coffee hoarders." So, we sat in that cheerful and cluttered kitchen, with its great aroma of freshly baked bread and stove-top coffee, and chatted—mother-daughter fashion.

Who had wanted to take music lessons, she asked me rhetorically. Of course, I had to admit it was my idea. Then she followed with another set of questions such as, "Who was sent to the library last month to represent the school in a book review contest?" "Who was regularly elected as a class officer" in the highly, highly moral elections where the good sisters told us we "had to elect someone of substance"? The answer, of course, to all these questions, was "me." Then she concluded with an idea that at eleven was totally new to me but would remain with me for a long time.

She said, "Your talents are not in music. If you ask me, they are with words and their use. We all have talents, and they are not the same. Be grateful to God that you have these and use them. I'll call Mrs. Scanlon and get you out of the recital—and music. It will be embarrassing at first, but this early I'm sure she can designate another child to take your place. Now forget about it." And she laughed again and told me that's what life was all about. You win and lose some, but it's not the end of the world.

I took the last slice of my homemade bread and final sip of coffee. Her hug said to me, "You'll make it dear. You have what it takes." How could I not with support like that?

How many times since have I thought of that? She was not just saying, "Buck up, you'll succeed at something else." She was saying, "You will find your own field, and you will be successful at it!" So, as I got a degree or submitted an article or encouraged a student, I have always thought that this was a valuable lesson this nurturing woman gave to me—and through me, to others.

XIII
Our World: A Retrospective

Middle childhood and early teens are the time for opening windows and doors and they certainly were that for me. In addition to my forays downtown by myself where my mother encouraged me to join the Fair Store rental library, which had much better books, I thought, than our local library and no age limitations, I was often invited to attend a girls' softball game where women's teams filled the gap caused by the draft. Mr. Gerrity, Alice's affable, quiet father, was a fan, and these games between the teams like Granite City Girls and Fresh Milkmaids were held at Shewbridge Field, built by and named for our pastor. Just recently, these commercially sponsored teams featuring players with typical names like "Granite Gertie" and "Walloping Wanda" have been honored by inclusion in the Cooperstown Baseball Hall of Fame, but to me they were just an exciting treat on an evening when my own parents almost always stayed at home. If I waited out in front, about two doors down, where the Gerritys would have to see me as they went out, I was almost always invited to be a pal to Alice who was five years younger than her closest sibling and who always accompanied her parents to these games.

Another world opened up for me when my brother Pat started high school at Campion, named for the Elizabethan Jesuit martyr, Edmund Campion, and located in Prairie du Chien, the second-oldest town in Wisconsin. The removal of distractions and concentration on studies and sports with the Jesuits appealed to my second-generation Irish-American parents, and my cousin Frank Riley, who had entered the Jesuit order a few months earlier, told them that the Jesuits were the best-educated educators.

Accordingly, Pat enrolled and we became frequent visitors. Since the students were allowed home only at Christmas and summer vacation, their lives seemed almost monastic, interrupted only occasionally for a trip to town to the dentist and a medical or family emergency journey to Chicago. The priests' surveillance and the "tight wraps" they kept on the campus were partially in response to the town of 4000, which had thirty taverns on its main street.

After the war started in 1941, the special trains we had taken were curtailed, but the Campion people always had a few train cars to themselves, and it all seemed very grown up and exciting. We took local cabs back and forth from the campus to the Old San Hotel or walked the two and a half miles when the urge dictated. Since the boys were not allowed into town on their own, there was much "feeding up" of sons on these trips, and that included lots of meals out, something our family was not prone to. I have vivid memories of steaks as tough as shoe leather during the war, drowned in A-1 steak sauce, a condiment unknown to our family heretofore.

One incident engraved itself upon my memory from that period. A group of teen-agers from "across the river" in McGregor, Iowa, was out one Saturday night and decided to come over to Wisconsin, possibly because Iowa at that place was "dry" and Wisconsin was not. They had missed a turn in the road and had driven their station wagon into the river. Next day, having heard the terrible news in the hotel, and having prayed for them at the Sunday morning Mass at Campion, my brother and I were more than ready when the news circulated around the hotel that their bodies were being brought back to town.

With the slightly ghoulish curiosity and total lack of self-consciousness of the young, we stood outside the Prairie du Chien mortuary and watched them take the six bodies in. The faces were covered, but the girls' legs stand out in my memory. They were all wearing the white snowshoes which were the precursors of our later popular shoe-boots and these stuck out stiff and poignant in that 1942 cold January sun.

Campion meant other things, like wonderful, teenage boys who were so much nicer to me than my own brother, I thought, and Thanksgiving dinners at St. Mary's, the girls school run by the School Sisters of Notre Dame, later beloved by me at Longwood. It was this same brother who was wearing the uniform of the Cadet Colonel and leading his "troops" in a dress parade while my father whispered contrary commands to the lines that were nearest us. Finally, it was a wonderful sense of family away from home which I was not to experience again until I found the sodality at Loyola.

When Pat graduated from Campion in 1944, I was also graduating from St. Leo grade school and going "out in the world." Though eighth-grade classes regularly made a trip to Riverview, famed amusement park on the North Side of Chicago, we "street savvy" children had already made that pilgrimage often on streetcars and buses.

We chose, instead, to have a banquet, and I was to give a speech—an address to classmates, the pastor, and our teachers who would be attending. My father, irreverent as always, offered me $100, big money in those times, if I gave the speech that he would write for me. I knew it would contain vivid descriptions of the conditions of the lavatories at St. Leo. They were beyond imagination in their appeals to sight and smell, and a description of them in the decorated auditorium where our banquet was to be held only a few hundred feet from their actuality was almost too much. So I declined the $100 and perhaps a chance at notoriety in my small South Side enclave of St. Leo. Had I given the speech exposing the condition of Msgr. Shewbridge's school plant, the echoing agreement of St. Leo graduates past and current might have sung out. Though some of my father's iconoclastic remarks had found a home within me, I hoped for life after St. Leo and knew somehow that the glee of a moment was not worth the cost of my many happy St. Leo associations and memories.

The fact that a child would gladly abuse his intestines and suffer inestimable pain in order not to visit the school bathroom seems ridiculous in retrospect, but the common experience can bring tears and laughter to the eyes of any two St. Leo graduates whose conversation ever strays into that area. Monsignor Shewbridge was famous not only for Shewbridge Field, home of girls baseball and the Leo Lions, but also for the seldom-visited "facilities" of his plant.

XIV
Longwood and Liberation*

To a young girl who had spent the first fourteen years of her life in St. Leo's parish and eight of them in St. Leo's very parochial school, going off to the Academy of Our Lady was akin to arriving at Oxford. Here were people who believed that I had a mind to be stimulated rather than a set of lessons to be covered. This is not to minimize the excellent foundation we received in arithmetic and grammar at St. Leo's. In third grade I remember memorizing my multiplication tables under the tutelage of a very young nun who happily passed out shiny satin ribbons to those of us who could recite them. Mine said "Queen of the tables" and despite my father's teasing as to whether that meant I could eat the most, I was proud of it. The next week, however, the much-feared principal, Sister Irma Therese, visited our class and took away all of our badges until we would know our times tables mixed up.

Grammar was treated with similar seriousness and, in those days of the intact classroom, if one had a teacher who liked grammar, one might well have it from the 8:45 bell in the morning to the sound of John Philip Sousa's march at the piano in the hall played by Alice or the McMahon sisters at noon. But, now, high school was different, with classes and even buildings to change. Longwood (the popular nickname of the Academy of Our Lady because of its location in a neighborhood formerly a suburb by the train stop called Longwood Manor) was staffed by a German order called the School Sisters of Notre Dame whose motherhouse was in Milwaukee and whose schools still dot rural Wisconsin like beacons on a trail. When I was a senior, I was asked to write an essay about their early days; I read that their foundress had cautioned her followers, "Speak more to God of your

---

* See also Part Two, Chapter VIII, "Fifty Years Later."

children than to your children of God." I thought that was a great sentiment and felt that my teachers had observed it.

To Chicagoans, these sisters were mainly "outsiders," unlike the familiar Sisters of Mercy who had many local Chicago institutions including a big hospital where my brother and I had been born. The School Sisters of Notre Dame were "strict and unapproachable." But to us who were "their girls" they were wonderful docents, feared and loved in varying degrees, but always the center of life during those years.

Here I was to meet Sister Francine, moderator of the junior sodality who, even when her sodality officers were fifteen-year-old sophomores, "wise fools," as pedagogical wisdom dubbed us, gave us Maritain and Graham Greene and then discussed them with us. There was Sister Ewald, the dark-eyed Latin teacher, who told stories of the ill-tempered Achilles and the weeping Andromache mourning Hector and turned us on to mythology, something the grade school books of that era would have found "heathenish." Finally, there was Sister Hester Valentine, later a writer of note, and still a friend.

Granted we had our eccentrics like Sister Claude in senior "civics" class, the '40s term for American government, who insisted that we bring "truck paper" or scrap paper from our fathers' businesses to use for quizzes and required that one-half of the room consider the government problem from the perspective of capitalists while the other side played the role of communists. Even now, so many years later, I realize that some of these were "great" teachers and, after many years in the field myself, I know that one does not usually need the second hand on which to count these "greats." I remember that I had several.

Nowadays, feminists and others herald single-sex institutions as being the best ground for young women to develop leadership skills and confidence. Maybe that was a bonus I got at Longwood because I know that these magnificent women epitomized both. Later, when I taught there, I saw the limitations of some of their leaders' myopic view of the world. One principal, Sister Charitas, who did handwriting analyses for the mission party bazaars we had twice yearly and who was written up in the *Reader's Digest*, dismissed the entire lay board of trustees as unnecessary, the very year that St. Xavier College was inaugurating its plans for expansion to the Southwest Side. She, and others, were surprised to find that all of them, including Morgan Murphy Sr., Chairman of Commonwealth Edison, had been welcomed by the Sisters of Mercy at St. Xavier as the expanded Board of Trustees at that college.

But these were not matters to concern us students at Longwood who were spending our formative years with giants like Hester and Ewald. The sodality officers were in Sister Hester's English class immediately after lunch in second year. It was in an odd classroom right as one entered the administration building, and Sister Hester's seniors seemed fond of hanging around on the porch in back of this classroom which had been, no doubt, improvised in this seventy-five-year-old building. While we sat there in class, Sister Theresita of the large key ring and black ledger often came in and out of her room which lay behind one of the two doors in the wall of that room. Since she was the treasurer of the order, we fantasized that she was in there putting all of Longwood's money in big bags which we knew she counted and recounted.

Within this classroom, known as 112 A.B., some intensive writing went on. A little sleepy from lunch, we would arrive to see an open-ended sentence on the blackboard such as: "A strange feeling came over me as I mounted the stairs. It was almost a foreboding, but I did not know of what until I opened the door and saw . . . ." Our assignment would be to write for fifteen minutes, after which we would go on with the class. The amazing thing, even to us sophomores who thought our teachers had no better things to do than hang on our words, is that Sister Hester would read what we wrote and give us feedback the very next day. It wasn't a nit-picking parsing of sentences. It was a genuine response to what we had said.

If she really liked the way we wrote, she'd add "Finish this for the *Longwood News*" or "Send this to *Today*—they would be interested." *Today* was a newspaper which, with a few other key Chicago schools' support, Sister Hester had helped to establish. It was edited by two talented young veterans, John Cogley and James O'Gara, under the sponsorship of CISCA, the Chicago Inter-Student Catholic Action organization headed by Father Carrabine. We groused and complained about Sister Hester's constant writing pressure, but we loved it when we got those messages. Several of us went on to careers which leaned heavily on professional writing. Sister Hester was a dynamic, beautiful woman who could not have been much past her early thirties at the time; she seemed to us a woman of the world and we would do almost anything to be "on her train." Hers was a heady diet which consisted of large doses of reading people like Dorothy Day and Graham Greene, discussing their ideas at Saturday meetings of CISCA, and doing good works.

She, supported by Sister Philemon the principal, brought speakers to Longwood like the controversial Carol Jackson, editor of the "back to the land" publication, *Integrity*. She also knew Ann Harrington of Friendship House, the interracial Catholic center in Chicago, who stirred our youthful idealism with the possibilities of society's reform. I was sent, with one or two others, to an evening series of summer lectures by the Baroness Catherine de Hueck who had escaped the Bolsheviks in Russia, we were told, and who later established a center in Canada for spiritual renewal with her famed *Chicago Daily News* husband Eddie Doherty of *Gall and Honey* fame.

These were times of great challenge. When I was starting college a couple of years later, I recall having to be gently persuaded through letters by Sister Hester that I would have a great deal more to offer the world if I got my college degree first. As prefect at the sodality for the senior year before I graduated high school, I had a chance to know Sister Hester better and to serve as city-wide ticket chairman of the CISCA variety show. People who know my difficulty at handling details like theatre tickets shudder to think that it was my job to seat the entire Civic Opera House. I was able to do it because my family and my experiences at Longwood had empowered me, as it is described in today's vocabulary.

The Longwood experience marked us forever. When I read some of Agnes Repplier's stories of her convent days, they struck a familiar note, but ours were far more than a sheltered period before real life began. We recall them even today as the beginning of our womanhood.

XV
A Thanksgiving with Dorothy

Though raised in a middle-class neighborhood where second and third-generation Irish-Americans predominated, our family had its own rather radical social views for that time. When I was graduating from Longwood, I remember going with a group from CISCA (the Chicago Inter-Student Catholic Action organization) to help rehab a house on 47th Street so that it would be livable. My family had no objection to my doing this, especially since Jim Milord, the twenty-three-year-old boyfriend and soon-to-be husband of my close friend Pat Johnson, would be with us.

I remember one day many of the streets were blocked for the Bud Billiken parade which went down Michigan and Indiana Avenues. Seeing these sights of a non-Irish America was a "first" for me.

Voicing beliefs in racial equality was not deemed prudent nor was it popular in 1948, so my parents, who could easily have been silent accepters of the status quo, surprised me. I suspect that my children today will find that their parents harbor many ideas that are neither traditional nor, in their vernacular, "square."

My parents' acceptance of the Gospel's message went beyond merely passive acceptance of what might have been dismissed as the enthusiasms of their eighteen-year-old daughter. One day at the Shamrock Beauty Parlor, which my mother patronized, a fellow patron made a disparaging remark about a black domestic whom one of the other women had working for her. It included generalizations about race that offended my mother. Mother rebuked the woman for her racial stereotypes. My father, brother, and I, hearing the story at the dinner table, hardly recognized gentle Genevieve, our soft-spoken mother whose greatest quality we knew to be tenderness. But as she said, it was a matter of principle that afternoon in the Shamrock.

I saw that quality in my mother a number of times when she saw an injustice had been done. It enabled me to imagine that the girl who had taught at the prim and precise Rubicam's Business College and Roofing Company could have been a powerhouse in a different time. Oh, how we often see things through our own narrow vision. Sometimes, a "Shamrock" moment gives us a clearer sense of the real.

A year or so later, my mother, father, and I made a trip to New York City over the Thanksgiving holiday. Thanksgiving trips had become a family tradition since my brother's days at Campion. They were opportunities for my father to give my mother a surcease from family obligations, and that holiday fortuitously coincided with a slow period at Chicago Granitine. Father Carrabine, a Jesuit who later married Ed and me and whom I had come to know through CISCA, had invited us to visit him at the Catholic Worker House in New York where he would be giving a retreat. My parents, who loved this good and humble man, were delighted, and off we went to the famous "House on Mott Street," located next to the teeming garment district.

We gave the address to a cab driver, who immediately asked, "Are you sure that you want to go there?" We knew what he meant when the trip proved to be interminable as the cab had to stop several times because racks of clothes were being trundled down the street between the various garment centers—all part of the distribution process.

So on we rode. My mother would have loved to meet Dorothy Day. She had recently read and was deeply moved by the autobiographical *The Long Loneliness*. When we arrived, we went up the steep steps to a clean but cluttered room where a beautiful woman, who looked like an older Madonna of Raphael, greeted us and said that Father Carrabine was in a conference. She offered my mother a bench—the apparent means of relaxation in that Spartan environment. As I looked at the gray heads in close conversation, I knew that Sister Hester was right, "Beauty is not only exclusive to the very young; it can't even be found there very often."

When Father Carrabine emerged, he said, "I see that you have already met Dorothy." That was when we realized that we were talking to Dorothy Day, founder, with Peter Maurin, of *The Catholic Worker*, active pacifist, and gatherer of people who had established Worker houses across the United States. She was subsequently regarded by many as an American saint and a woman who could speak lovingly to all whatever the circumstances.

We attended Father Carrabine's conference that day, and the visitors from Chicago were warmly welcomed and more than felt at home. Father Carrabine must have known that my mother and father would fit in perfectly in that Christian world. We saw a few people in business attire, but most of these were the Catholic Worker staff or conference participants who looked like they might have belonged outside the mission.

My father told me later that one of the men he chatted with that night reminded him of the man he had hired on the unemployment line during the Depression and who was now foreman of the shop. My dad chatted with this New Yorker and clearly felt that they were two working men, one for the moment without a job and one who by God's grace had started a job at seventeen and now at fifty-plus was president of the company. Dad clearly felt they had much to exchange.

We always remember the extraordinary things in our lives rather than the stuff we did every day, but when I think of my mother and father today, I often see them taking a pamphlet at the Catholic Worker House that Thanksgiving—or telling that cab driver, "Yes! That's where we want to go!"

We went back to the Statler Hotel that night and had a great Thanksgiving dinner and saw friends of my father the next day. The memory that lasts though is the sweet time that Dad and Mom shared with Dorothy and her friends at the Catholic Worker.

XVI
The Marquette Moment

In September of 1948, I left Chicago to attend Marquette University. Harry Truman was to be elected president in November—an election upsetting the political predictors and seen by a number of people on television for the first time, if not in their own homes then at a local bar or in the homes of more affluent friends. I had become eighteen and the world was out there. I had not yet learned the lesson, which life teaches us several times over but not permanently, that what one imagines something to be is not always the way it is.

I did not want to go to Mount Mary, which I pictured as just a continuation of Longwood, staffed also by the School Sisters of Notre Dame. Wonderful as my high school years had been, I was ready for something different. I did not want to join several of my friends who were going to travel an hour and forty-five minutes twice daily to Mundelein, located at 6500 North on Sheridan Road. But Marquette, a Jesuit university located in Milwaukee just ninety miles north, had been coed for a number of years, was Catholic, and would provide me just the atmosphere which my desire for independence and individuality required. Hadn't I been allowed—almost sent—downtown alone at age ten? Hadn't I made new friends from all over in my role as treasurer of CISCA, the Chicago Inter-Student Catholic Action organization, and later as the ticket chairman of the variety show held at cavernous Civic Opera House? Surely Marquette and I were meant for each other. I couldn't have been more wrong.

I have never analyzed all the reaons why my single semester at Marquette was so painful, but certainly one cause was that I was paired up with a roommate who was a junior in Journalism and who regarded her presence at Marquette as the most acceptable means of escape from Sun Prairie, Wisconsin. I have since thought that while I was eighteen, going on nineteen, she was twenty going on thirty-five. She chain-smoked, had all her classes scheduled from noon on, and never started studying until midnight—with the ceiling light on at all times.

As the only girl in my family I had always had a room of my own, and my very considerate small family would never have thought of making noise after someone else had gone to bed. Here as a freshman, I had classes daily at 8:00 a.m., and I always went to Mass first—to give me strength, it later devloped, to stand the rest of the day. So I was up and out of the dorm by 6:30 a.m., having slept about three hours. As a lowly freshman, I didn't dare complain at the nocturnal habits of my roommate. I was being a "good girl," a role which had always served me well, and I had no reason to think this situation required something different.

Thirty years later, my daughter, Mary Kate, at seventeen and a lonely freshman at Yale, was able to challenge one of her three roommates within weeks after she arrived at New Haven. The roommate, Emily Rose, had moved in after the others, was already on the staff of the *Yale Daily News*, and had received three phone calls while she was in the shower one night when the others were already in bed. When Emily returned, the three girls were waiting for her with Mary Kate as the spokesman, reading the "riot act" regarding phone calls after their agreed-upon curfew. The calls stopped and the four remained close friends. Was it the thirty years that had elapsed between her college experience and mine or was it that my daughter had a much firmer hold on her priorities and a better grasp of what she needed to survive? I suspect the latter.

The converted apartment building called "Alumnae Hall," which was my home at Marquette, was presided over by a former WAC Sergeant who ran it as she had her troops, and dinner at night at tables of six was an eminently grim affair for me. One had to leave the library right on time; otherwise, the dining room door was closed. I didn't have the charm or authority to command the dinner table conversation, and I found it so different from the table presided over by my mother who just might have received a letter from her St. Louis family that day or my funny father who probably had met someone outlandish that day on a trip to Drovers Bank. These dinner companions were not interested in me—the Chicago freshman—

who was so serious about her work or—little did they know—was scared to death that she was not going to "make it" in college. One junior from De Pere (was everyone from small towns in Wisconsin?) who sensed the tension within me once told me that I was trying too hard to be nice.

My classes did nothing to reassure me that all was well. I had been steered into a trigonometry class for which I did not have the prerequisite and I was positive I was going to fail. Indeed, I would have failed, had it not been for Sister Mechtilde at Longwood and her visiting priest-brother who coached me over the Christmas holidays. Semester exams occurred at the end of January in those days, and their help enabled me to pass.

As for Latin which the famous Father George Ganss taught, I found myself far behind Marquette High School graduates. My Longwood experience with the warm Sister Ewald, who was to help me so much four years later as a freshman teacher, had emphasized the wonderful mythology behind the classics rather than grammar. I can still hear her describing the doomed Hector saying goodbye to his weeping wife Andromache. Now I was faced with translating Livy who Father Ganss said wrote like the ancient equivalent of *Time* magazine. But, with work, I could make up my deficiency, and I surely was ready to work.

When I found that even my English teacher, a graduate assistant, didn't like my writing, I despaired. She had gone to the "never use the passive voice and that's all you need to know" school, and did not like my more baroque style. But since I had more confidence in this discipline than in math or classical languages, I felt that this rejection was not devastating. I needed help and my classmates who went home nightly to loving Polish or German families were in a different world.

Not even my father's jocular letters helped; notes with checks urging me to eat heartily "because I like my gals with plumpish curves," and to "get yourself good, red-blooded meat early and often," or reminding me that "a check from home" required only an "ask and you shall receive," were to no avail.

At Thanksgiving, I saw by chance (or is anything by chance?) Eleanor Zoeller, a high school friend who had been president of our senior class and who, with one or two others, had gone straight to the downtown campus of Loyola University where women had been admitted for only the last couple of years. She told me that Loyola was a good place to be, and I was ready to hear her message. "No," she said, "it is not just a men's school with a few girls allowed in." Rather, "it is like the real world with people of all different ages and races and faiths in one building and we love it."

Returning to Marquette after Thanksgiving, I started making arrangements to transfer at the end of the semester, and the first glimmer of hope lightened my life. I don't remember much about the end of the semester, but I do know that I would not have emerged sane had I tried to tough it out for the whole school year. The old saying about "knowing when to hold 'em, and knowing when to fold 'em" certainly applied to me. I transferred to Loyola in February of 1949. Though I was not in a position to know it then, I had found my home.

XVII
Loyola

Those years at Loyola's Lewis Towers, February 1949 to June 1952, compared to my exile in Milwaukee, were a heady experience full of new friends, satisfying classes, and stimulating experiences to a girl whose Chicago-phile father had sent her off downtown at age ten. Now, a lover of the City myself, I boarded the "L" at 63rd and Halsted. It later went underground to become a subway at Roosevelt Road and took me to the near-North-Side location of Loyola situated at what is now called Water Tower Place. The university occupied the first nine floors of a tall brown building, which had been used by the navy during World War II, called Tower Hall. Now owned by philanthropist Frank J. Lewis, it held students rather than midshipmen, for he gave the first nine floors to Loyola for its use but reserved the upper eight floors for the Illinois Club for Catholic Women, an interest of his wife, Julia Deal Lewis. Mrs. Lewis was very much alive and present at club affairs and we sometimes saw her ample fur-clad frame in the club rooms upstairs on the rare occasions when we students got up there. Part of her philosophy was to provide housing for single young Catholic women living in Chicago, so certain floors were residential. The first eight floors of the building were Loyola's undergraduate classrooms and offices, and the ninth floor was the law school. Later on upon Mrs. Lewis's death, the entire building became Loyola's.

The people I met in class were not unfriendly! One of them, Mary Kay Heintz (now Lynch), sat next to me in Spanish class, where we were the only two girls, and she took me one day to the "Sodality Room," actually the office of Father Joseph F. Hogan, student counselor and Sodality moderator who was to play such a big role in my life and remains a dear friend today. Just back from service overseas, Officer Major Hogan eschewed office-type aggrandizements. A wooden desk in one corner, with a telephone on top, a number of student chairs, a blackboard, and three coat racks completed the furnishings. These he made available for any students who wandered in. Loyola students had no lockers in those days, so the coat and book racks were always overflowing, and that cold day in my new school there were people perched at all angles, conferring over assignments or having spirited discussions of a point just covered in a Philosophy class or eating lunch. Father Hogan thrived on it all, and messages were hastily written on the blackboard by whoever picked up the phone. One ingenious arrangement was a confessional next to the room which could be entered from the backstairs. When the penitent came in, he rang a little bell inside it and the bell resounded in the sodality office. If Father Hogan was in, he immediately entered the confessional from his side of the hall, and if he was out, a chorus of voices notified the person waiting. We often joked that someone could commit a murder on Rush Street, climb the three flights of stairs to Father Hogan's confessional, and be back out on the street before the body had been discovered.

Years as a soldier's chaplain had taught Father Hogan that you don't push religion at people, and he was always ready for a discussion, but never poised to point the finger at a man trying to get his education and life in order after fighting a war. His inauguration of outdoor Masses at the beginning of Sodality picnics was a carry-over from service and his way of combining fun and liturgical feasting. Some of the people from those Sodality Room days still regularly seek him out for counseling and always celebrate his birthday which comes at the end of January. This continues a tradition that began with his birthday fortuitously coinciding with the end of the semester. This was campus ministry at its peak and, somehow, seeing other people in our lives as Christ was a lot easier after we had practiced on our varied brethren in the Sodality Room. There was always someone there to talk to, go to lunch with, or get help from.

Friendships were forged and long-time marriages bloomed in this spot which I learned from Father's fellow Jesuits was called "Hogan's playpen." Serious confidential sessions in that more informal age, Father took upstairs to the bar in the Catholic Women's Club. What a wonderful time!

In addition to the "club room," the Sodality had an organizational structure which held meetings on Fridays after the compulsory student Mass at the cathedral, two blocks away. On First Fridays we had a breakfast served at the Ranch Restaurant on Oak Street. I arrived there the first time, only to find a group who all seemed to know one another, already eating and chatting. Chester Koziol, figuring up the group's bill at a table near the door, spotted my tentative entry and found me a place at a table where he knew I would be made to feel at home. He was my knight in shining armor forever.

We had everything, we thought, in that building settled between Michigan and Rush, across from what was to become Bonwit Teller. My speech class was presided over by the young but poised Mariette le Blanc, whose father was a professor of French and who was able to deftly silence a classmate wanting to tell us for the third time in his class presentations how to go AWOL in Paris. It was not a surprise that she later became the first dean of women and then vice-president of the university. Though there were not many young women, we all came to know one another in places like the second floor washroom, presided over by Tony, the Matron, who always had an aspirin or a shoulder to cry on. Years later, when I was teaching there on Saturday, I hung my coat in that washroom and was absolutely flabbergasted to find it stolen when I finished class. I was reluctant to admit that the world had changed since 1949.

So complete were our lives within the building that it was possible to come in for an 8:00 a.m. class, work at Montgomery Ward's later in the day, and return for an evening class, finding one's pile of books in that same corner of Room 319. There was no sharp distinction between day and night students, for as one became a junior or a senior, he often had to get a course in his major in the evening. The fledgling campus was hardly elegant but very serviceable. Father Ralph Gallagher, the genial sociologist, made frequent tours to the basement lounge where in addition to rancid sandwiches, there always were at least six tables of pinochle, the game of choice, going on.

When Mary Kay Heintz and I realized on April 13, 1949 that we were both celebrating our birthdays, we treated ourselves to a lunch across the street at Yonkers and began a birthday tradition which we, with our husbands, keep today. Next door was Old Cathay, the pro-

17 ~ Loyola

prietors of which were blessed by Father Hogan, who frequently happened in there and impressed them with his brand of Christianity.

In that building for the next three and a half years, I was to meet sardonic but kind Joe Wolff, who taught us History of English Lit. at 8:15 three mornings a week. On Thursdays, in preparation for our Monday test, he gave mumbled hints down into his collar which we wouldn't miss for anything. Dr. D. Herbert Abel also intrigued us with his pipe-chewing pronoucements on the Nibelungenlied in a course called "Classical Epics."

I found surcease from a bad case of scruples which had developed at Marquette, with the curmudgeonly Father Charles Doyle, one of the first priest-psychologists who combined European study and local roots and for whom the Doyle Center at Loyola was posthumously named.

There were dramatic moments in class when Father Norman Weyand, English department chairman, would soar into song while reading English ballads. The word in the university was that if ever stuck for an answer with Father Weyand, who had written the biography of modern poet Gerard Manley Hopkins, one might invoke the name of Weyand's beloved poet. While taking my master's orals several years later, that occasion arose. My mind went blank when the questioner asked if I had ever heard of "sprung rhythm." I ventured that it was particularly associated with Hopkins. My hide was saved, and he congratulated me on my perspicacity.

The entire experience at Loyola, Lewis Towers, was a happy one where I studied, partied, made cakes for historical society meetings, and thought I was in love at least twice. As Eleanor had said when I talked to her in 1948, it was the "place to be."

How much my happiness at Loyola was conditioned by my lack of the same at Marquette, I do not know. I had discovered my people, and this was home.

XVIII
The Remarkable Aunt Mary

"I'm Aunt Mary!" exploded the booming voice all the way down the stairwell in the outer hall at Green Street when my husband-to-be, then my date, Ed, rang the bell to pick me up in November of 1956. On our second date, my parents were away, having taken the train to New York where we were to spend Thanksgiving, so Aunt Mary was in charge. And Mrs. Full-charge she could seem, fresh from retirement at Rubicam's very respectable Business College in St Louis where she also "manned" the office at the Rubicam Roofing Company. Ed told me later that if he had not been quite interested in courting me, that greeting would have sent him packing. I suspect that might have been the effect she had on students at Rubicam's where she taught bookkeeping. After all, this was the school portrayed in Tennessee Williams's *Glass Menagerie*, where Laura, modeled on Williams's sister Rose, was scolded for her late arrival at class and never returned there again, unbeknownst to her mother, Amanda, who was trying to secure her daughter's future. Mary Travers was born the first child of James and Elizabeth Shanley Travers in the last decade of the nineteenth century. James's mother had died on ship while the family was coming to America from Ireland, so when James later married Elizabeth in St. Louis, his rather intimidating father, for long years unsoftened by the presence of a wife, would often call on the young couple.

There's a picture at my cousin Betty's in Arcadia, Missouri, of Aunt Mary, a beautiful little girl with long brown wavy hair flanked by her two younger brothers, Joe and Jim, the Travers children who preceded my mother. It must have been taken around the time when their Grandfather Travers paid them surprise visits. The story goes that once they didn't have time to escape to the yard so they hid under the round table with the long cloth to the floor, customary at that time and again favored by designers today. While their young mother hastily prepared a repast for her father-in-law, perhaps she wondered why the children were so quiet, but, hustling around, she put it out of her mind until she saw a horrified expression come over the grandfather's face. Looking around, she must have seen the table with the long cover, moving, making its way to the door. The cover, of course, was swept off, and we can imagine what happened then. It must have been six-year-old Mary who masterminded it, for Joe at four and Jim at three could hardly have been so devious. Mary's mischievousness never left her and even though she ran a "tight ship" in her classroom at Rubicam's, the capacity to enjoy a joke surfaced regularly, even when the joke was on her.

When I was about ten and my brother thirteen, Aunt Mary spent a period of several months with us to recover from an illness, and we gave her quite a send-off. We had one of those two-headed rubber masks which were introduced in the 1940s, and ours represented a derelict who looked both depraved and diseased. My brother Pat donned an old robe and this head, and came up the steps of this same stairwell through which my Aunt Mary later called down to my future husband, "I'm Aunt Mary." I was to buzz Pat in through the outer door and leave the inner one to our flat unlatched. He ascended the stairs and all went as planned until Mary suddenly opened her bedroom door, just opposite the front one, and beheld this Dorian Gray-like apparition. She screamed and tried to get away, but he advanced faster. The "inside man" in this nefarious plot, I began to panic when I saw my aunt grow breathless in her attempted escape and I remembered the heart condition, the amelioration of which was the reason for her extended visit. By the time I had reassured my mother, who had joined the hysterical group upon hearing her sister's screams, Aunt Mary had dissolved into laughter and pronounced it the funniest trick ever, much to my brother's and my relief. Not so easily placated was my mother, who relaxed a little when she realized her sister was O.K., but lectured us sternly on the possible danger to Aunt Mary. She was right, of course, but we were ten and thirteen, and our relish of the joke far surpassed our remorse.

When Mary was seven years old, my mother was born, and the bond between the two sisters, which carried to their graves, was forged. Together they nursed their mother, who ultimately died at forty-six of pernicious anemia, through her last two years, mixing equal doses of prayer and ministration. They chose middy blouses, went to lunch, and shared friends. The Travers girls were a close twosome. Mary was already working at Rubicam's when her mother died. She married Frank Riley in 1916 and had two children, Frank in 1917 and Betty in 1918.

When Betty and I took a wonderful trip in 1953 to Ireland to trace our shared roots, we found an old woman in County Leitrim who remembered that her aunt had once received a letter from America which said that Mary was to marry a man named Frank Riley whose sisters Mary and Genevieve already knew. It was a happy but sadly brief marriage, for Frank Riley succumbed to the flu epidemic of 1918, dying on one floor while his wife and new baby daughter were on another. He was part of the statistics in what my historian husband has labeled the largely unreported pandemic of the twentieth century. So Mary spent most of her motherhood alone, though extended family, in those days of more mortality, rallied round. My widowed grandfather and single mother moved in with Mary and that sharing of Betty's and Frank's babyhood led, I am sure, to the close relationship my brother and I always had with our older St. Louis cousins. Aunt Mary's house was where our grandfather lived until his death in 1939, and the base from which we could get to know all our St. Louis cousins over the years.

Indeed, my mother averred, we might not be in existence if it weren't for Aunt Mary. When my mother and dad met at a summer resort in Michigan, it seemed unlikely that this romance would end in marriage, given the geography of the times and the family responsibility each one felt. After a period of years during which my father made several (ostensibly business) trips to St. Louis and charmed all my mother's nieces and nephews with his toilet paper draping and adult-baiting jokes, the romance seemed stalled. So Mary took action. "Well, Gen," she said, "if you are discouraging that nice Bob Grogan from Chicago because of the children and me, you are making a big mistake. Having him in the family would be an asset." My mother evidently took her sister's advice seriously and on September 30, 1925, Genevieve Travers and Robert Grogan were married in St. Louis. Seven-year-old Betty was flowergirl, and there commenced an alliance closer than just a cousinly one. Betty became my father's favorite, and an older sister to me.

Mary had returned to work at Rubicam's when the children went to school, and remained there until her retirement many years later. As my godmother, she indulged me with smocked dresses and tearoom lunches, and made her high-ceilinged three-floor house available as our St. Louis "home away from home." Her regular trips to Chicago, supplemented by periods of recovery from illnesses and month-long stays after her retirement, enabled me to know this funny, courageous lady well.

During World War II, she took me with her one time to visit Betty, recently married to Bud Murphy, who was soon drafted but allowed to live off-base in Houston. I was twelve and big for my age and my aunt was never thin. But we shared a berth on that long train ride and I'll never forget almost bouncing into the aisle when Mary let out one of her snores or snorts. Again, when I was graduating from high school, Aunt Mary was planning to visit her son Frank, his wife, and two babies in Mexico City, and my parents gave me the same trip as a graduation present. When I demurred about flying, my aunt said, "Well, you can go any way you please but I'm flying." We shared a great trip and I remember my chubby, spunky aunt riding on a burro down a cobblestone street in Taxco, Mexico.

As she had taken me, she took each one of her grandchildren on trips back and forth from Texas to Missouri so that her two children's families came to know each other well, and they all remember her with her hearty laugh, often joined by a shaking stomach. Aunt Mary raised single parenthood to a high art in an era when the term was scarcely used, but we will always remember her as the lady who called down our cavernous hallway, "I'm Aunt Mary," and who managed to be mother, aunt, and grandmother with a flair.

XIX
Maybe Teaching:
An Exploratory Foray

"Did you teach at Longwood in the 1950s?"—the woman asked as she rushed out of the stockroom of the flower shop where I was ordering a plant in the early 1980s. "Why, yes, but how did you ever know that?" I asked the proprietress whose window arrangements had attracted me with their unusual detail. "Well, I was in your Junior English class and I could just hear you again giving us the assignment to read the next act of *Macbeth* or write a paper on some current problem. We knew we were breaking you in, but you really turned some of us on." And so it had happened again. My identity as the teacher had caught up with me—and not unpleasantly in this case for she remembered fondly her days at the top of the red brick administration building at the Academy of Our Lady, my own high school, to which I returned for my first three years of teaching after graduation from Loyola in 1952.

How I came to be there was either a matter of angelic intervention or happenstance, depending upon your point of view. I always knew my English major would lead to something, though I knew not what, and the principal's call in February of the year I would get my bachelor's degree was not quite Gabriel, the messenger angel, but solid evidence that this was indeed my mission. I had somehow always thought of teaching as going into a kindergarten, a role for which I had no eagerness nor aptitude, but teaching high school girls, at my very own beloved Academy of Our Lady, who would be eager to share my love for the English classics and my delight over studying them—well, that was different. "But," I objected, "I have not taken any education courses. Won't that be a problem?" "No," the principal opined, "I think you'll find that our structure supports the new teacher quite well, and you may even pick up a few ideas from your colleagues here, many of them your former teachers. But if you have any time in your remaining semester it might be a good idea to take a few education classes."

That was all I needed to hear. I had been delayed from a February graduation by, the summer before, a ruptured appendix which, had it not been for the discovery of penicillin, might have cost me my life. What it meant was that I had only a couple of credits to complete and was free otherwise to register for whatever I wanted. I signed up for four education courses and only one necessary course in English, venturing out of my hallowed discipline into the department variously known for "busy work" or a "super-structure imposed on common sense." I learned nothing that was useful to me later, but met people who, while they professed to be unlocking the secrets of teaching, were actually violating all the principles thereof. Any real instruction in how to teach came from people like the Utopian scholar Father Edward Surtz who later was tragically killed in a biking accident, or the dramatic Father Norman Weyand, who had written the book *Immortal Diamond* on the Jesuit poet and developer of modern poetry, Gerard Manley Hopkins. Then there was the bibliography professor, John Webster Spargo, who in spite of his great deformity caused by an automobile accident met us standing in Cudahy Library each Saturday morning, admonishing us that our shoes were much too shiny, for it was shoe leather we really needed. He taught the course as though we were fledgling detectives, sent out to solve a particularly brutal murder, savoring our triumphs in discovering whether Rousseau and Voltaire were both really on the European continent in a certain year, as had been mentioned in one's letters.

Though most of the education classes had been useless, educational philosophy with Father Gleeson had given a panoramic view of the varying ideas people had had on this profession I had "fallen" into, and I felt that a stint in the classroom was in order before I went to Longwood. So I signed up for supervised student teaching the summer after graduation and was assigned to a public high school in a blue-collar neighborhood a few miles east of where I lived. My students were not making up courses they had failed, but were attempting to graduate a semester early, getting a jump on their entry into the world of work. I found that these juniors and seniors already knew not only what jobs they would hold in the factory or assembly plant after high school graduation, but what year they would be able to retire and begin their real lives. Since these students were just five years younger than I, I have often wondered how this era of change in the marketplace affected them. Did their companies merge with others, forcing them into early retirement, not an unwelcome thing considering their views, or, less welcome, into a change of jobs at age forty or fifty, requiring skills and flexibility I wasn't sure they had? I remember Robert M. Hutchins, Chancellor of the University of Chicago, warning an automation-hungry populace that teaching people what buttons to push was not the kind of education they needed because within a few years, the buttons would be changed. My summer at Hirsch High School was not unmitigated joy. My students did the assignments dutifully if without much eagerness.

One day I finally found a story in our literature book which would, I thought, "turn them on." It was about the people in a town who got into a municipal dispute over whether to give to a local beggar who regularly asked for hand-outs as they left the town meetings. Remembering the back-porch diners of the '30s and how impressed my father always was when hobos offered to do some work after eating, I could see the point of view of those who said the bum should get a job in that rather high-employment post-war era, but I had also known enough people, even a friend of Aunt Bessie's whose inability to hold a regular paying job had been caused by invisible emotional problems, finally leading her to suicide, that I could not just conclude that this man should work rather than beg. The students read the story and the ensuing discussion became more lively and finally heated. I was delighted. It was possible to rouse these passive students.

When my morning class was over, the critic teacher, who spent most of his time making arrangements for his photography business, approached me with a frown. "Miss Grogan," he began, "it is not a good idea to get the students all 'riled up' like that; you lose control. Since I was there, no harm was done but . . . ." I was deflated, but could do nothing. The principal, Mrs. Goldie, encountered me later when she saw me passing her office with a despairing look on my

19 — Maybe Teaching: An Exploratory Foray

face and coaxed the story out of me. "Oh well," she said, "you'll find your own style—and change it as you learn."* I suspected she was a wise woman later that week when one of the other student teachers, a blond with a beautiful figure, said to her, "Oh, Mrs. Goldie, all the boys want to date me—what am I to do?" "Well," Mrs. Goldie responded with a scowl, "that is something I do have an answer for. Time will take care of that."

As the summer ended and I prepared for my first "real" job at Longwood, I did not realize that in the experience at Hirsch, I had glimpsed how good it could get—this profession I was so blithely entering—and how bleak it could seem when professional jealousy and apathy and sheer incompetence could almost drive one out. My profession had and still has the best and the worst among those who claim it. The floral shop lady who remembered my voice awakened a memory of both and of the hint of immortality with which it seduces.

---

* Cf. Part Two, Chapter XXX, on Mary Jane's later thoughts on one's style.

XX
Ireland and Longwood

When Sister Theodora greeted the junior classes that September, she came as close to warmth as this very ascetic principal could muster when she said, "And teaching junior English and with the homeroom 301 A.B., we have our own Mary Jane Grogan who has returned to us to begin her career." It was a gracious gesture from the woman who had sent me a business-like letter a month before which said, "Our motherhouse authorizes us to pay beginning teachers $4,328 per school year. You will teach five classes of Junior English, be responsible for a homeroom, and participate in all school activities related to your teaching." So! This was my mission from Gabriel and I accepted it.

I had already enrolled in two graduate English classes, and these, along with preparation for teaching, were to keep me busier than I could ever imagine. But I was reluctant to leave Loyola with its combination of happy student days and the social contacts it provided, feeling that I was "furthering" myself by pursuing, even part-time, a master's degree. Life was full and though many of my friends, especially close ones like Marion Gleason, for whom I was maid of honor in August 1952, were starting off on their life choices, I felt that could wait a while. Once I got over being rejected by the fellow I had seriously dated in my senior year, when his former love came back from the convent she had entered, I threw myself into my work. My father's wonderful humor and kind way of laughing at things helped me to do so by frequent references to romance, always coupled with the idea that there were other fish in the pond. And there were, for my graduate classes and that wonderful haven up the backstairs from Rush Street, the Sodality office presided over by Father Hogan, provided as many social contacts as my life as a fledgling teacher and graduate student could accommodate.

20 ~ Ireland & Longwood

I had always wanted to see Ireland, and my Aunt Bessie Grogan had corresponded with her aunt by marriage, Mrs. Margaret Padden, widow of my great-uncle Michael who had been my grandmother's brother. I'll never forget asking advice from Father Weyand, the colorful English department chairman and biographer of Jesuit poet Gerard Manley Hopkins. If I took a trip to Ireland, I confessed, that would preclude any graduate classes that summer, and I really did want to get my master's degree sometime. Father Weyand looked at me with that sardonic half smile he often wore, replying, "Graduate classes will be here, Mary Jane. This moment to visit Ireland may never come again." So, after one year of teaching, I took all that I had earned from that parochial school salary they paid me and started to plan a trip. My father, true to form, was enjoying this trip vicariously and suggested that he sponsor my first cousin and beloved friend Betty Murphy who was raising children and helping her husband start a dairy in Arcadia, Missouri, one hundred miles south of St. Louis. My Aunt Mary had already retired from her work teaching at Rubicam's and with a longish visit from my mother, my father said, the St. Louis people would get along just fine. So Betty and I flew to New York and then to Shannon in mid-June on a trip which remains a precious jewel in my memory of those early 1950s. Spurred by a priest friend, Father Kenneth Hoffman, who had given memorable retreats at Longwood, we extended our trip to include London (still decorated after the coronation of the young Queen Elizabeth), Paris, Lourdes, and Rome, returning on the *Andrea Doria*, that beautiful but ill-fated ship, in July.

My first year at Longwood had been hardly triumphant, for I looked a little too much like the students I was teaching, but I made it with advice from Sister Ewald, camaraderie from Sister Francele, a youngish nun who would mount the steep stairs to my third-floor classroom on the days I didn't have classes at Loyola, and an occasional compliment from one of my most obstreperous students who stayed after school one day to say, "I bet you could have been a writer—or even a stewardess. How come you decided to teach us?" In those days the strict height, weight, and appearance requirements made it hard to qualify as a flight attendant. So her question implied a grudging approval, an appreciation of other possibilities, and pleased me. I didn't answer that the angel Gabriel had planned it all.

The Academy of Our Lady had not changed much in the years I had been gone. It had been a boarding school in the late nineteenth century and had evolved naturally into a large girls' parochial high school. But I had changed a great deal; I thought that I could truly take my place on the other side of the desk with no problem. I forgot that people of sixteen and seventeen often feel they have outgrown the authoritativeness which their parents and teachers still feel they can exert over them. None of the challenges to my authority were serious ones. I realize that now when I hear of shootings in classrooms and intimidation of students by gangs in public schools today, but to someone new at the game they could be quite daunting.

One student, for instance, always ate her sandwich in class during the 11:30 period right before lunch and I knew it was undermining my control of the class. I had spoken to her a couple of times, but one day it really got under my skin. We were reading *Macbeth* aloud, the students taking the various parts, so I waited for her to take a bite before calling on her to read. When she couldn't speak, I commented sweetly, "Oh, that's right, it's not polite to speak with your mouth full." I got my laugh and with it the grudging respect of the sixteen-year olds who were ready to challenge my authority.

I stayed two more years at Longwood while finishing my master's degree at Loyola. During that time, I developed some coping skills which I hadn't known were there, learning from women like Mary Cahill who was the veteran dedicated lay teacher across the table from me at lunch and Sister Mona for whom I was designated "prudent companion" so that she could attend Loyola's evening school. I had on-the-job training. When I talk occasionally with first-year teachers from National-Louis University, where I teach, about their loneliness and pressure in that first job, I remember my own. The longest journey one ever takes is that step from the student's side of the desk to the teacher's. Before that change, one knows what everybody thinks about the course, the teacher, the tests, and the grades. Once that exchange has been made, one knows nothing. The extraordinary women who assisted me those years made an indelible impression. They were the universalists G. K. Chesterton had described. Two principals following the ascetic and unworldly Sister Theodora, Sisters Fortunata and Seraphia Marie, became my champions and rejoiced with me when I got my master's degree. Little did they know that they had given me guidance and modeling that I could never have gotten in a class. They were my true education.

XXI
A Last Glance at Ethnicity
and Irish Catholicism

Father Andrew Greeley has made parish identification in Chicago famous in his many sociological and fictional works, and its presence was a big factor in the '30s, '40s, and '50s. Most of us had attended the parochial grade school—for me it was St. Leo's—and on Sundays my father even dutifully drove us to the 9:00 a.m. "children's Mass" where we sat with our class while the adults had to go into an annex. To many, that was an example of an over-controlling clergy who feared that our infinitely conscientious Irish Puritan parents wouldn't make sure that we got to church on Sunday. We just accepted it as normal and were glad to pile our friends into my dad's Oldsmobile after church, hearing them laugh at his jokes about the sermon and utterly amazed at the questions he would ask about friends' fathers' jobs and the parishes their parents had come from, queries which might have sounded impertinent from anyone else but which, with my dad's great good humor, were merely expressions of interest.

Although we St. Leo scholars ended up knowing all the early fathers of the church and could recite not only the ten commandments but the precepts, the beatitudes, the gifts and fruits of the Holy Spirit, and the seven deadly sins, more emphasis was placed on rote learning than on seeing how these might impact our lives, as was indicated in our unconscious ostracizing of our eighth-grade Croatian classmate, Nelly.

The pastor, Monsignor Shewbridge, could be formidable, but in the manner of recent presidents, loved to be folksy at large gatherings and, we learned later, supported an unemployed brother who had never gotten established in life. The principal, Sister Irma Therese, was dignified and demanding of St. Leo boys and girls but was also very proud of those of us who had received our educational foundation there. While learning was not exciting, it was solid, and our teachers, who mingled little in the community, went back to Terre Haute, Indiana every summer for courses at the motherhouse which led them eventually to the degrees they didn't have.

Later on, being from St. Leo became both less and more important. My high school teachers at the Academy of Our Lady were far better educated and opened true intellectual doors, but St. Leo's remains the place which had nurtured me and where I was married in 1958. It was now no longer under the direction of Msgr. Shewbridge, but the bailiwick of Father Pat Molloy, also known as "pay as you go" Molloy, who had eradicated the debt incurred by the high school building and stadium Msgr. Shewbridge had constructed.

According to Margery Frisbie's well-researched *An Alley in Chicago*, the acclaimed story of Father John Egan, priest of Chicago who instituted or participated in every ground-breading Catholic action movement beginning in the late '30s, Monsignor Pat Molloy had been the confidant or go-between of the Capone and Bugsy Moran gangs in the 1920s. She writes of the time when a considerable sum of money was missing from an envelope being passed between the two groups. Cardinal Mundelein, the "shepherd" of the Chicago archdiocese who merited the title "builder cardinal" for his erection of St. Mary of the Lake Seminary and many other edifices, received an anonymous phone call saying that unless P.J. Molloy was out of the country by that night, he would be at the bottom of the Chicago River by morning. Pat Molloy was sent to Argentina to do missionary work, returning only years later when the reasons for the city's worldwide gangster reputation were a part of history and legend.

Now, in 1958, he was pastor at St. Leo, and my father, ever a practical man, didn't want to upset him by unexpected traffic congestion at our wedding the following Saturday. According to Dad, the conversation went something like this: *Dad:* "Monsignor, I think we might have quite a few people at my daughter's wedding on Saturday and I wondered if you thought we might need some help." *Monsignor Pat:* "Why Mr. Grogan, we have big weddings and funerals here all the time. A couple hundred people here do not seem to bother anyone." *Dad:* "Well you see my daughter and her husband are in their late twenties and early thirties. They have both taught at as well as attended several schools. There might be a number of Jesuits from

Loyola here and even some former students from all over the city. I was thinking more in terms of six or seven hundred. I'll see that you are reimbursed for any expense you might incur." *Monsignor Molloy:* "Oh, that won't be necessary, Mr. Grogan. You see, I happen to know the police captain pretty well, and I think a phone call from me . . . ." Dad was realizing that parishes built in the 1920s did not have parking lots and police did not take well to clogged streets.

Needless to say, there were police on hand that Saturday to assist us out of the limousine and see that all went well. Father Molloy turned up later at the reception at South Shore Country Club to give a long, rambling greeting. After reading in Margery Frisbie's book Father Egan's description of a police-escorted trip to Comiskey Park with Msgr. Molloy many years before, I am hardly surprised that it needed only a phone call from him to prevent the traffic problem. His predecessor had difficulty pressuring people who had suffered through the Depression to give more than their usual contribution. Monsignor Molloy, who had started out as a boxer, did not have that problem. Had he been around when I gave my eighth grade speech in 1944, I'm sure my father would not have tempted me to rail against the latrines; they would have been replaced. As it was, he successfully restored the parish to solvency and we, the parishioners, never dreamed how close our blunt, raw-edged pastor had come to feeding the fishes in that long-ago time, now celebrated in the famous movie, *Bugsy*, starring Warren Beatty and Annette Bening.

So, Father Greeley was correct in emphasizing people's identifying themselves with a parish in Chicago, but this may have been lost in the greater mobility of the late '80s and '90s, along with the secularization of the present day. Coming from St. Sabina's or Visitation or Christ the King was a bond which was a combined result of the parochial school system and the strong family identification with the Church. That it will ever be duplicated in this age is unlikely, and there are many who will not mourn its passing. I hope that its loss will not be a vacuum, but rather an opportunity to embrace greater variety so that an eighth-grade Nelly Smajo will not be made to feel strange because of her babushka and pointed shoes. But, given the ethnic tensions recently resurrected in Europe and the ability of people to form exclusive groups, that may be more a dream than a reality.

XXII
The CYO Detour

After teaching for three years at Longwood and acquiring my master's degree, I was ready for a change. Endless papers from my students and for my professors seemed to be a permanent part of my life. I was sure that other people went to work at nine and left at five or six without thereafter ever giving their daytime work a thought. I spoke to my friend, Father Joe Hogan, about it. "Let me talk to John Hayes," he offered; John Hayes was the president of the Archdiocesan Council of Catholic Men and dean of Loyola's Law School. I had seen him in the lobby at Lewis Towers and possibly even shared an elevator with him as he had ascended to his office on the ninth floor, one floor above that of Father Doyle whom I still stopped in to see almost every week.

John Hayes and Joe Hogan had gone to St. Ignatius Grade School together and then on to Loyola Academy. When John continued on to college at Loyola, Joe Hogan entered the Jesuit seminary, but they had remained fast friends and saw each other often. When Major Joe Hogan came back to Loyola from his army chaplaincy, Hayes and Hogan were often seen with their heads together.

Thanks to Father Hogan's intercession when I went to Hayes's office, at Father Hogan's direction, I met not only John Hayes, but two men whom I was to see frequently in the next year while I temporarily switched careers from teacher to youth worker: Matt Gobreski, office manager at the Catholic Youth Organization and a prince of a man, and Gene Kent, editor of the publications of the Mission of Our Lady of Mercy.

Mercy was known to many Chicagoans as the Working Boys' Home. Msgr. Kelly, with the assistance of Kent, mounted eloquent appeals for help for these boys, providing a good-sized envelope for donations. In the 1950s, many people did not have checking accounts and they stuffed change and dollar bills into these envelopes, sending them off to the Home or the office of the CYO. Once those were received at the CYO office, it was the job each morning of retired Sears Executive Joe Gladstone to slit open these envelopes and total the money. Sometimes there were poignant messages down with the pennies and nickels about someone's childhood on the street or heartrending requests for prayers which he duly noted and reported. After a long and successful career at Sears, Joe thought he would be giving something back by this contributed service. He became a good friend.

Anyway, John Hayes, along with Gobreski and Kent, told me of a new plan about to be launched by the CYO which sounded to me like a network of discussion groups through the parishes for which I would be directly responsible. I was excited and they offered me the job of Supervisor of Girls Activities on the spot. With the recommendation from Father's childhood friend and head of all the Holy Name Societies in the archdiocese, the "fix" was in.

Bishop Bernard J. Sheil, auxiliary bishop of Chicago, with considerable publicity had launched the Sheil School of Social Studies, a center for adult Catholic education, some years before. Now this was to be his foray into the parishes. Since the CYO already existed, why not channel it through that organization? Accordingly, I gave my notice at the Academy of Our Lady and began a year's stint at the CYO. One of my duties was to put out a monthly newsletter, and another was to give talks at communion breakfasts and evening gatherings at parishes.

Unfortunately, Bishop Sheil's network of discussion groups never became a reality and most of my duties centered around appearances at athletic events where I would smile and comment only on the people there, not the sports played. My immediate boss at the CYO turned out to be Tony Malcak whom I had known from early sodality days at Loyola. Tony had left evening school at Loyola to get a physical education degree at DePaul. He taught physical education one day each week and directed the program at the CYO the rest of the time. Tony never told me that he had been shocked at how little I knew of actual sports, but when he complimented me on how I always knew just the right thing to say to the nuns and the brothers, I took the hint.

One Sunday each month the "professional staff" had to take turns going to the CYO office, receiving the scores from the Catholic leagues, and phoning them to the *Tribune*. My dear friend Leona Reynolds volunteered to accompany me to what we thought would be a dark office at 1122 South Wabash that first Sunday afternoon. When we arrived, we found two hundred Chicagoans from the Philippines having a meeting and party there. They wanted us to join them, so I explained that we had to be near the phones, but their warmth and inclusiveness remain with me today.

I remember too how Tony and Matt Gobreski used to stop by my office on Fridays on their way to the Berghoff bar where they would enjoy a fish sandwich. It was a "men only" place and they would invite me to come along and then, in mock recollection, say, "Oh, that's right, Mary Jane, women aren't allowed there." Matt died far too soon, but Tony and I reminisced one time about their Friday ritual. I reminded him that the Berghoff bar was one of the very first places to be "crashed" by women in the late '70s when such restrictions were found to be unlawful. I learned that year that working alongside men required a kind of cooperation and camaraderie which was laced with humor and punctuated by allusions to sports figures and tournaments I had to pretend to catch. I didn't know then that I would have a husband and four sons in the future who would teach me about these things.

There were all kinds of people at the CYO, and I learned that year how hard it can be for a young professional to give necessary orders to the secretarial staff. I learned also that people in offices often had to stay late or take work home, just as did teachers. Ann Graham, my Aunt Bessie's Irish "Roomer" and lifelong friend, was good enough to ride with me to remote parishes for evening talks, but I found that I seldom saw again the members of groups I talked to. The contact was not a close and binding one and, to my surprise, I missed teaching. Just to make sure that I was not romanticizing the classroom, I offered to teach the junior English classes at Longwood of my former colleague, Mary Joan Stegman, while she went on her honeymoon with Dr. Charlie Range who had gotten his M.D. when I received my master's the preceding June. The relief I felt at getting up for class those four mornings rather than preparing to go to the CYO convinced me that, indeed, I belonged in teaching. Since that day in early 1956, I have never doubted it again. Teaching is the ultimate opportunity to be in touch with a person in the part of him that is basic—his hopes and dreams. I began planning my departure from the CYO.

XXIII
ST. XAVIER

By the end of 1955 I knew that I wanted to resume my teaching career. I had talked generally about my decision to my dear friend at Mt. Mary in Milwaukee, Sister Mary Chrysostom, at Christmas. The following February I was asked to join that faculty. I hesitated. I would be in Milwaukee—again. Sister did urge me to come. But I decided to explore things locally. Fortunately. For this was going to be truly the year of Providence: Doubt on January 1, 1956—engagement to be married, December 31, 1956. But an entirely different life if I had accepted the position in Milwaukee.

Just how I was going to get back into teaching was a mystery to me. I had met Sister Josetta Butler, then President of St. Xavier College, whose family lived across the street from mine on Green Street, when she visited her father, but I did not know her well. However, beginning to glimpse the fact that it was through people that one got an entry to anything, I decided to use my slim connection. Everyone who knew the proud history of the Sisters of Mercy in Chicago, the builders of the first hospital and later the college called St. Xavier, had heard that this, Chicago's oldest college, was moving from 49th and Cottage Grove Avenue to 103rd and Central Park. Hadn't the city just changed its boundaries to include the College and thus make it eligible for city services? The new buildings were under construction and the expanded facilities would certainly require an expanded staff.

So I swallowed my Catholic schoolgirl timidity with its attendant "speak when you are spoken to" attitude, partially overcome in the male atmosphere of the CYO, and called Sister Josetta. She was, until her death in early 1995, gracious and dynamic. After inquiring as to whether I had the use of a car that day, she invited me to call on her that very evening. Thanking my Irish luck and my boss, Tony Malcak, who had asked me to stop at one of the CYO vacation schools that morning, thus necessitating that I have the car, I agreed.

Sister Josetta received me in one of the parlors at St. Xavier with the windows open upon a scene of urban blight. The furnishings were old but comfortable, not looking for a minute like the convent parlor described by Joe Dever in his short story "Fifty Missions." Dever had depicted there a young man's visit to his former girlfriend at the convent which she had entered while he was away in service and which was marked by the high-backed chairs and the grandfather clock on the wall, ticking away the minutes of his life as he waited for her to appear in her new role.

Sister Josetta was large—physically and psychically—and she set about to find out everything about me that night. Had I really enjoyed teaching? Was I sure that I wanted to return? When she discovered that I had a special interest in writing and had an article published in *America* on my experiences as a lay teacher in a Catholic school, her eyes twinkled. I would be released from one course every term at St. Xavier to fulfill my duties as faculty sponsor of the *Xavierite*, school newspaper of the college. In high school, I had written only an occasional article for the school paper and had no idea what a job it would be to train reporters, editing their work and supervising them in the paste-up of the newspaper. So I naively agreed, but even if I had realized how little I knew and how much there was to it, I probably would have jumped at the chance. That was how eager I was to get into college teaching.

Attending a summer institute at Siena High School after leaving the CYO, I was introduced to the St. Xavier plan of education and met several of the faculty whom I came to respect as fine educators and deep thinkers. They were very anxious, these fine people, to provide a continuum between their old St. Xavier College at 49th and Cottage Grove and their new quarters at 103rd and Central Park, out in the "boonies." At 49th in the shadow of the University of Chicago, students and faculty were able to share colloquia and maintain a relationship which was unique in higher education. In my two years at St. Xavier, I was able to sense that closeness and benefit from it with Sister Benoit who, my friend Jean McAndrews claimed, always spoke in Shakespearean English, telling her students that it was "a consummation devoutly to be wished" that they hand in their papers. Then there were Sister Consilia, another great English teacher, and Sister Mary of the Angels who sent students off to the public schools with confidence. They, along with Dominican priests from the House of Studies in River Forest, made up a highly intellectual but warm and friendly group who were to be my friends and colleagues for the next two years.

The first time that I went to one of their meetings in the school cafeteria on the new campus, I felt that I had happened into a ladies' social or bingo party, so convivial was their demeanor. They were far different from the School Sisters of Notre Dame at Longwood. Though my first allegiance will always be to the more reserved school sisters, I came to respect these women immensely.

There was Sister Anacleta who was embracing the technological revolution before any of the rest of us knew it had happened. In her office at the end of my hall where I was given a room that doubled as the *Xavierite* press room, Sister Anacleta played teacher to two of Mayor Richard Daley's sons two nights each week when they would be delivered by limousine and picked up a couple of hours later. When she heard that I had a dinner date one night with her newspaperman nephew, she decided to favor me with a demonstration of all the technology which her studio contained. She was a veritable encyclopedia of old Chicago whose history she delivered with a salty touch.

Sister Antonine, who headed the speech department and years after took on our son Joseph's speech impediment at age three and four, became a friend also and remains so today. After determining that Joseph's problems were not neurological and working with him for some months, she confronted me one day with the following diagnosis. "This is a very bright child. He doesn't want to do all these tongue exercises unless he sees that they have a purpose. Get him into school." On that word only, we started him at Morgan Park Academy four months before his fifth birthday. When I watched him give the valedictory address at St. Ignatius, thirteen years later, I thanked my lucky stars for such a friend. How many children are subjected to "readiness testing" by an impersonal examiner and categorized by someone who has no real knowledge of what makes them tick?

My mentor at St. Xavier was a mature lady, Mrs. Lucas, who asked me one day what I thought of the curriculum course called "Critical

Analysis" which was St. Xavier's version of English 101. Thinking of the many scientific articles which made up the curriculum and which I found hard to read, I answered that it was "quite thorough but rather dull." Mrs. Lucas and I often went down to lunch together, but she didn't stop for me for the remainder of that week. Sensing a strain, I asked her directly on Friday, "Have I offended you in some way?" Her eyes became iridescent as she replied, "Do you know what the word 'dull' means? It means mindless, stupid, without life." My heart sank for I realized that I would never be able to erase from her mind the offhand comment that I had made. If that course was dull or stupid, then its creator must have been the same. That creator was Mary Ehrie Lucas, sometimes called by the students, irreverently, "eerie Lucas." That single incident brought home to me that the connotations of a word are at least as important as the actual meaning. Mrs. Lucas was courteous to me, but I don't think I was ever truly forgiven for my *faux pas*.

Hardly had the term begun when I received a fateful phone call from Father Norman Weyand, Chairman of the Loyola English department. He asked me to teach two courses in Loyola's University College and when I demurred, saying I had just begun my first college job, he added, "Oh do it for a few weeks." So new was I to college teaching that I thought that might be possible. Besides, wasn't this the man who had been an important part of my master's program and who had been a revered mentor and friend? Thus began my years of teaching part-time at Loyola, which would extend through the early years of marriage and children and up through most of the '80s.

It was also to lead to my meeting my husband, Edmund Kearney, in the late summer of 1956. I was with Sister Hester at the Newberry Library, scene of many graduate students' research and where I had written my master's thesis. Just outside the Newberry was Washington Square, also known as "Bughouse Square," a place where political orators, religious preachers, and snake oil vendors gave speeches by day and early evening. Sister Hester, now a faculty member at Mount Mary College, was in town for the day, and I seized any such opportunity to take her around and share her thoughts. We had been looking at the files at Newberry where a few years previously I had

23 ~ St. Xavier

been introduced to "Mr. Kearney, our teacher" by one of my younger friends, Vera Zivny. Sister Hester and I did not find what she needed at Newberry so we went downstairs to the cloakroom to use the one phone which the burghers of this fortress-like edifice allowed. I volunteered to call Chicago's Public Library to further pursue a text she wanted, and was surprised to see "Mr. Kearney" outside my phone booth. "Did he remember that we had met?" I fretted. Or was I just a bothersome body preventing him from making his call. I took a chance and greeted him, introducing him to Sister Hester.

There must have been some magic in the air that day, or our guardian angels were taking their missions very seriously, because he appeared again a few weeks later when I stopped into the English department office to pick up copies of the syllabus for my class. He was chatting with Jack Clark, who had been a doctoral candidate when I was seeking a master's degree, and we had been in a few classes together. I also had shared the summer institute for St. Xavier with Jack's mother-in-law, Mrs. Holden. I never knew how long Ed had been waiting there but he later said he had been there for a while. We greeted and made small talk about running into each other again. The very next day my phone rang and it was Ed Kearney. He was going back to Cleveland, where he taught history, but invited me to dinner and a concert the very first weekend he would be back in town. To this day, Ed loves to say that when he asked me if I liked Wagner, I asked what position he played.

I don't remember it that way and if Tony Malcak had been around he would have said that I knew as little of sports as of music. Since people do not fall in love because of their shared knowledge of either, those two meetings must have been providential.

XXIV
Providence:
Courtship and Engagement

After meeting Ed Kearney, first at Newberry Library and then in the English department office, our romance progressed rapidly. Getting a long distance call from Cleveland, where he taught at John Carroll University, to set up a date for a future weekend was indeed flattering, and when he began to call every Thursday, I knew he was serious. I had seen him many times at Newberry across the reading room presided over by a woman we grad students called "The Gauleiter" after Hitler's enforcement guards. If anyone ever said more than three words to another person within the reading room itself, she wagged her finger and hissed "Shhh."

But silently observing the young man who came and went to the desk in the reading room, I thought he had very kind eyes behind his horn-rimmed glasses. Further than that, a properly brought up young lady would never have gone. Having been introduced to him by one of his own students, who was also a friend of mine, in 1951 or '52, made it all proper. So years later when Sister Hester and I found *Mr.* Kearney waiting to use the telephone and when I encountered him a couple of weeks later in the English department office, it surely seemed to be fate. We look upon it as Providence and regularly thank God for our own special expression of God's love and care. Perhaps he sent an angel (on whose feast day, The Guardian Angel, Ed was born in 1925) to facilitate the contact, but the realization of our providential meeting has been an ever-present reminder that the hairs of our head are indeed numbered and not a sparrow falls that it is not noted by the creator.

Ed and I had a wonderful night on that first date, at a little restaurant called Mario's on Van Buren, followed by the Wagner concert, and then dessert at Lander's next to the Palmer House. It was a warm November 1 and when we came home via the "L" and bus, Ed gallantly offered to turn off the hose, saving my parents the trip from the second floor. The fact that the dampening of his clothes with the spray from the leaking faucet did not seem to do the same to his spirits reassured me of his intentions, and I resigned myself to wait for his next visit to Chicago which was to be right before Thanksgiving. On that date, we went to a party at Jack and Mary Ellen Clark's house, but I still could not bring myself to tell this young man that I had a car, since he was so obviously without one. Between November 1 and the end of the month, there had been one of those rapid changes of season so characteristic of Chicago and we were indeed cold while we came home, but I did not want to seem to be in charge of the plans by offering the car. Now, almost thirty-seven years and several aeons later, custom-wise, that seems ridiculous, but in 1956 it was very real. A young lady did not want to seem "over-eager," even if one was just that.

This many years later we have laughed over the roles that custom, tradition, and propriety played in the elaborate dance called courtship in those days. But I wonder if current young people aren't bound by as tight a rope as we were. One time I suggested that one of our children go out on a casual date with someone, only to be told that people don't do that any more unless they intend to get serious. How can one get to know a number of people who might be marriage possibilities if one doesn't go out with several? Certainly the number of guys that I went out with in the late '40s and early '50s didn't feel that I had led them along falsely, I hope. Indeed, dealing with many Loyola undergrad and grad school classmates had enabled me to get to know people on a person-to-person basis without the complication of boy meets girl arrangements.

My mother and father, never travelers, except for forays to St. Louis, had begun to take short trips over Thanksgiving, a time when Dad could get away, and I was always included in their plans. So the next day after our cold but wonderful date, I flew off to join my parents in New York for the four-day Thanksgiving weekend. I flew back Sunday since I had to be back at school Monday, and hardly was I home, when Mary Ellen Clark phoned to say that Ed Kearney's father had died suddenly over the Thanksgiving weekend. Remembering how Ed had said that he and his father planned to have dinner at a restaurant on the holiday and visit his mother who was in a long-term hospitalization at Wesley Memorial Hospital, I was shocked and hastened to attend the wake where I would get the only glimpse of the man who would have been my father-in-law.

John Kearney had been a member of the 1st Division commanded by Colonel Robert R. McCormick, editor and publisher of the *Chicago Tribune* and distinctly isolationist in his views. The memorial museum of the 1st Division remains at Cantigny, west of Chicago, the McCormick estate open to the public.

After World War I, John had been in the Army of Occupation and had spent several years in France before returning to Chicago where he met and married Mary Dinneen in 1924, Ed being born a little less than a year later. John Kearney was ten years older than his young wife, and she may have been surprised at the occasional hard drinking sprees that he went on—no doubt relics of his war years. But his job as a pressman was always secure, and after a heart attack in his fifties when he spent a long time in Hines Hospital he was a model of sobriety. He had had a hard childhood before the army, as the oldest boy of five children whose mother had died young and whose father was not known for his stability. He lived with relatives for a time, was in the Working Boys Home for a while, and finally had fended for himself on the streets of Chicago. His sudden death must have been a terrible shock to his wife, Mary Dinneen Kearney, whose slow-healing bone surgery confined her to the hospital for many months and prevented her from attending the funeral.

At the wake, I invited Ed to visit our home after "all of this is over," and he suggested the next night, after the funeral. We both knew that ours had not been merely a casual date. He came the night of the funeral and later in the week took me to meet his mother, still hospitalized. Then Ed returned to John Carroll University for the month of December.

Just before Christmas that year, my cousin, Betty Murphy, always like an older sister to me, had her fifth child and only son. Betty had complicated pregnancies because of the Rh blood factor, about which little was known in those days, and all of her children had been delivered by Caesarean section, early. This meant a longer hospitalization and sometimes a complete blood change for the infant who, in this case, had been rushed to St. Louis for treatment. The wonderful little hospital, St. Mary's, felt it did not have the facilities to care for this high-risk infant. So, one of the sisters and Betty's husband, Bud Murphy, had ridden the ambulance to St. Louis to give Patrick Murphy his chance at life.

Knowing that Betty's mother, Aunt Mary Riley, had signs of the heart condition which caused her death in 1963, I offered to go to Arcadia, Missouri to help out. Betty's four little girls ranged in age from Martha, who was two and a half, to Ann, my god-child, almost ten. During that time, I told Bud Murphy, Betty's husband, about the new man in my life, and he enlisted in the campaign to get me back to Chicago while there was still something of the vacation left.

Ann, my god-child, must have heard the end of one of her father's and my conversations because she said to me one night, "Janie, if you get married, could I be your junior bridesmaid?" I responded by asking her how old she thought a junior bridesmaid ought to be. "Oh, thirteen or twelve or eleven or ten," she answered without hesitation. She was covering herself for sure, and when she walked down the aisle a year and a half later, I knew that she belonged there.

So I came back on one of the last days of December 1956, and Ed proposed that New Year's Eve on the Grogan couch at 8146 Green St. When I told my parents in the morning, my mother was delighted and my father wanted to know what I knew about "the guy." Starry-eyed, I could understand my father's concern, and I promised to ask people at Loyola. I began with Father Hogan. Knowing that Ed had received his Ph.D. in History at Loyola a year and a half earlier, he immediately thought of his childhood friend Paul Lietz, Chairman of the History Department. Fortunately for us, Dr. Lietz gave a glowing report about Ed, who had taught many courses at Loyola before taking the full-time job at John Carroll, and I was able to reassure my dad that this was a person of worth and stature to whom I was linking my whole future as well as the man I loved.

Though we were to have a number of problems and barriers strewn in our path before the final "I do's" on July 26, 1958, the future plans were settled. The fact that I would probably have to leave my Chicago home and begin a new life in Cleveland gave me some qualms, to be sure. But wasn't that what my mother had done over thirty years earlier when she left St. Louis to marry Bob Grogan? I knew that somehow it would work out.

XXV
THE FEAST OF ST. ANNE: JULY 26, 1958

The day, July 26, 1958, our wedding day, dawned clear and beautiful. I had been granted almost everything I could have wanted—St. Leo Church where I had been baptized and made my First Communion, a lovely place on the shore of Lake Michigan for the reception, and now a beautiful day. In 1958 when so many places were not yet air-conditioned, we were really gambling when we chose a July date. But Ed had to teach a summer session at John Carroll, so it had to be then.

Father Martin Carrabine, dear friend and founder of CISCA, Chicago's Inter-Student Catholic Action organization, had been doubtful about getting permission to come to Chicago for such an event, but a conveniently scheduled conference here had made it all possible. Though Father had advised professors, labor leaders, and seminarians in large numbers, he had not presided over many weddings and was quite nervous, probably more nervous than we were. What I had really hoped for happened—a full church where our former lives of relatives, neighbors, classmates, teachers, and friends would be together. Father Molloy, the pastor, was there, with the street where I had walked to the corner daily with the south ranks in grade school, blocked off.

There were many of our Loyola friends—Fathers Hogan, Bryant, and Finnegan along with Father Charles Johnston, the Dominican priest friend from St. Xavier. The charismatic Father Mike English was giving a retreat at the Longwood Cenacle but made an appearance at the country club, and I was thrilled to see later that day that Father Charles Doyle, the priest psychologist who had held me together when I struggled with scruples some years earlier, had come too. My parents, recognizing Father Doyle's appearance on a busy Saturday, put him next to them at their table. His curmudgeonly way and my father's wit went together well.

Mother and I had worried about having a large wedding after my dad's two heart attacks, and this made us decide not to display wedding gifts at home, a practice at that time guaranteed to bring a steady stream of traffic through the house. A particularly precious one from all the Riley and Murphy cousins was a Christmas crèche with figures designed by Bertha Hummel, member of the famed artist family who, as a nun, had been almost starved to death in Nazi Germany.

My dress was the first one I had set my eyes on at Bonwit Teller, across Pearson Street from Loyola. When I met my mother in March to choose it, we ran into the ascetic scholar and my revered teacher, Father Edward Surtz. My mother, not realizing, I thought, how uninterested he would be in such things, bubbled over about how we had just found a dress. Obviously, just as in the case of Father Stratman whom she had wooed with her lamb chops, Father Surtz was easily struck by her charm and entered wholeheartedly into a discussion of organdy and Dior hoops.

The veil, I knew, would be a simple extension of the little white sharkskin skull-cap given me five years previously in Rome by Pope Pius XII at the audience we had shared with a group of twelve. On that trip my cousin Betty had brought introductions to the Servite monastery in Rome which had provided us graciously with two young seminarians who took us all about Rome each morning, and they told us that in the religious goods stores near the Vatican, one could purchase such a cap or zucchetto. Then, if you were close enough to the Holy Father and held one of these in your hands, the Pope would exchange it for one he was wearing. Indeed, that was just what happened and when he blessed the hat, I imagined it as the basis for a wedding veil when I met the person I would want to spend my life with.

Now that day was here! Rather than being bothered by all the arrangements involved in a wedding, my father seemed to seize upon them as a challenge. He wanted to put kindred souls together and generally succeeded in the seating plan. Throughout the preparations and the day of the wedding, he was his affable self, offering just the right amount of iconoclastic commentary upon this ritual.

Because the organdy wedding dress was stuffed with tissue and hung in the back bedroom of my parents' house, somehow with all

25 ~ The Feast of St. Anne: July 26, 1958

the tissue, my gloves, small organdy mitts, were buried, and when the time came to leave for the church, they were lost. It didn't bother me a bit, but it upset my maid of honor, cousin Mary Lucille Grogan, to no end. I think she finally gave up trying to make a lady of me at that moment when I said, "Oh let's go, I always hated gloves." So many of my aunts and cousins from St. Louis and even my dearest male cousin Frank Riley and his wife Betty from Texas were able to be here that it made it a true family reunion. Betty and Bud Murphy brought their entire family of five children, including the oldest, Ann, my junior bridesmaid. One picture shows Aunt Mary at the front of a large group of relatives, looking for all the world like the burgomaster heading a delegation, and Ed says he is reminded every time he sees it of his introduction to her in November 1956 when he came to pick me up for our second date and she called down through the front hall, "I'm Aunt Mary . . . ."

Ray Cowan, our photographer, whom I had come to know through the work on the school paper at St. Xavier, exceeded my almost unreasonable request not to ask people to pose for pictures and yet came up with wonderful ones. When we had changed clothes and Bob Konen drove us to the hotel where we were staying before flying to Ireland, we could honestly say that we had enjoyed it all. I left my home and beloved parents where I had spent twenty-eight years, full of the fears that all brides have for the future, but with a real sense of joy. Ed's humorous request that now that the Jesuits had left we ought to have a Catholic ceremony brought a good laugh. With all our priest-friends, classmates, and students, as well as my two nieces, flowergirls Susan and Marianne Grogan, we had brought our past and a hint of our futures together. We did not know then that we would be blessed with five wonderful children of our own, but as I placed my bouquet at the Blessed Mother's altar, you can be sure that prayer was in my heart.

XXVI
Starting Out

The date for our wedding on the feast of St. Anne, Mary's Mother, July 26, 1958, was based on Ed's summer school schedule at John Carroll University. His good friend and apartment-mate Luis Soto-Ruiz gave a party for us in February of that year, and I went down to meet most of the people who would be our friends. The plan of living in Cleveland progressed, but my heart was heavy. My father had already had one heart attack, and I was not anxious to leave Chicago where my parents and all my associations had been. The five months in Milwaukee in 1948 were still a grim memory, but I assumed that starting out as a couple would be quite different from being a lonely freshman. My term as president of the Loyola Alumnae Association would be over, and I told them at St. Xavier that I would be leaving town and would not be teaching there next school year. In retrospect, that was a rather rash act, but remembering the late nights spent at the college working on the *Xavierite*, I thought that was no way to begin a marriage, even if by chance we would be here in Chicago.

Along about February, Ed contacted an old friend and teacher, Dr. Joseph Chada, to see if there might be a possibility of a position at Chicago Teachers College. Dr. Chada was encouraging. I took hope. Like Ruth in the Bible, I would follow my husband wherever he went, but all things being equal, it would certainly be better if the "Whither thou goest" could be right here in Chicago. Ed's mom, widowed recently, was another consideration.

Ed told me later that, with his historian's pessimism, he feared that if anything happened to my father, I would feel compelled to put off marriage, being the only child at home. I responded that he did not understand my mother Genevieve very well. Right after his proposal the Christmas before, Ed had reinjured his knee, perhaps weakened by the paralysis of his childhood, and this had led to a cellulitis infection and weeks of hospitalization including surgery. It had not been an auspicious beginning to our engagement and we often have said that it prepared us for the fact that one doesn't need flawless health for a happy marriage and family, but one does need a means of support.

So it was with enthusiasm that we greeted the offer of a teaching position for Ed at his undergraduate alma mater. He had gone there after graduating from Leo High School because it offered a college education for very little money—if one had just a little political clout. Ed knew that he did not want to teach grade school; indeed, the discipline of history was his forte—but this just might give an entry to this specialization. Everyone at Chicago Teachers majored in education, but it might be possible with hard work to have a second major like history. So after a visit to the alderman to seek his blessing, a necessary step in a Chicago just emerging from the Depression and politically tied to the Democratic party, Ed applied at Chicago Teachers College. Probably he would have been accepted anyway, but people didn't take any chances, so the alderman's visit was part of the ritual.

After graduating with a history major and teaching at St. Ignatius High School for a couple of years, Ed had gone full speed ahead toward a Ph.D. in history at Loyola, working as a graduate assistant and, ultimately, teaching many courses there. So that is how it had happened that I had observed the young man with the kind eyes across from me at Newberry Library and had been introduced to him by Vera Zivny, a fellow Loyolan who was a few years younger than I and who was his student. By the time we met again in 1956 at the telephone booth at Newberry with Sister Hester along, we had actually shared a graduation in 1955 when Ed was getting his doctorate and I was getting my master's.

We both remember being invited to take a "smoking break" at the Granada Theatre where Loyola graduations were held, while we waited for General Mark Clark, whose arrival had been delayed. In 1955, nobody had even remotely considered a connection between smoking and cancer. Though not smokers, Ed and I remember chatting with mutual friends in the parking lot. But that was still June 1955; we had a ways to go before November 1956. One might call it coincidence, and in a Greek play we might disparage it, but in real life that's the way it happened, and we consider it Providence.

So now after his surgery and a year of formal engagement while I worked at my job in the Alumnae Association, fulfilled my contract at St. Xavier, and taught in the evening at Loyola, we were married. I held on to my part-time teaching position at Loyola, and we hoped to start a family. Meanwhile, my father, encouraged by news of Ed's job in Chicago, did what he had done seven years earlier when my brother had gotten married. He bought a house and proceeded to negotiate a deal with Ed and me to rent it from him. As I suspected in my heart of hearts, Dad was putting the "rent" we paid in a fund to pay off the equity so that it would eventually be ours. And he had arranged that, in case of his death, which occurred less than two years later, just four weeks after Mary Kate was born, the house would be ours.

Every time my dad would stop at our house during that first year, ostensibly "to use the facilities," he would always bring something that new householders need—a mop, a broom, a bucket. R.S. was enjoying this as much as he would have if he were starting his own home again. So the man who had been in the business of supplying homeowners with house accessories such as laundry tubs and alley-opening garbage boxes but who had never built his own house was going into ownership again, vicariously. R.S. was always in the business of empowering others, it seems to me even this many years later.

XXVII
Beginnings

I suspect the first year of marriage is hard for everyone, but in different ways. For me, struggling to get my thank-you notes done (I really made a project of them, writing, in many cases, long letters which I am sure now were neither necessary nor appreciated), getting the house furnished, and getting adjusted to Ed's hours, which were so unlike my father's, constituted a full-time but not always fulfilling job. When I heard the local school children return home from St. Walter's or Sheldon, I wondered if we would have voices like that in our house. Would life be more than sometimes picking up Ed, either at the Teachers College at 69th and Stewart or his transfer point at 71st and Western?

I tried to get used to my new husband's tastes which were not very complicated. We both remember one incident which, in retrospect and considering all the real problems people have, seems funny. I had fixed a pear and cottage cheese salad to accompany the main course at dinner, and I was quite proud of it. Ed consumed it with gusto and then remarked off-handedly, "You know what's really good too? Pear in lime jello." I was crushed and must have shown it because later in the evening I remember Ed's telling me how sorry he was for his thoughtlessness. Ah, such were the problems of newly marrieds!

Other uncertainties arose, such as whether the same doctor who had given Ed problems as a student about certification would possibly block him again. We kept close contact with both our parents and yet tried to be totally "on our own." I think we both felt that we were waiting for real life to start. Ed had to prepare for a written test, because he would be certified by the Board of Education, and the material he was perusing seemed to have a lot more to do with educational theories than with history.

We discovered, as Ed likes to say, that we were basically incompatible and, after that, things got a whole lot easier. I was a people person who liked to have many friends and associates, while he was far more selective and apt to lose contact with people if they didn't nurture the relationship. Though I had come from a family that lived hardly on a grand scale, that was more by choice than necessity. Ed's family kept things carefully, preserving them fastidiously. A number of his childhood toys like a tank brought him by his Aunt Margaret's boyfriend who died tragically attest to that. When we were unpacking our wedding crystal, a Dutch design, I broke one or two sherbet dishes. I rubbed my hands together and said, "Well that's two that we won't have to worry about."

Ed was genuinely shocked that I brushed it off so blithely, and I wasn't about to tell him then that a few years before I had gone through a worry period when such accidents would have upset me a lot. I had learned that things can always be replaced, an attitude he teases me about today.

I was teaching only on Saturdays at Loyola, and the idea was that we would have our family almost immediately. When I didn't get pregnant right away, I wrote to Father Carrabine in Cleveland who referred me to the priest who presided over Catholic Charities, and I made an appointment for both of us. To his credit Ed, though considerably less enthusiastic than I, realized how important children were to me and agreed to go along. The priest reminded me ever so gently that we had been married only a matter of months, and promised to keep our adoption application "just in case." As we looked over our brood a few years later, we laughed about this and appreciated his courteous treatment.

At the time of the Christmas holidays we had an open house for some of the many people who had given us lovely wedding gifts. We were settled for an unlimited time, we thought. We had no idea that within four years, our life would be changed radically, and we would make another move. Ed was considerably more accustomed to moving than I, for the Kearneys had lived in a number of places, in and around St. Carthage parish, and now his mother resided in a lovely

27 – Beginnings

flat in a building owned by the Lavezzis just one mile west of my own family. We often reminisced over the fact that after our first date, I had said how sorry I was that he had to go home to another part of the city. He laughed and informed me that he was a lifelong South Sider himself. I lived in the same house to which I had come from Mercy Hospital in 1930, and thought he resided, as did most Loyolans, up North.

As spring came, I grew restless, waiting to get pregnant, and I filled out an application to be a substitute at the Board of Education. Certain signs indicated that I might be pregnant, and I remember confiding that to the very understanding Board of Ed doctor who conducted my physical. She wanted me to jump a certain number of times and I said I'd rather not. She let it go at that, bless her. Meanwhile, my father had had another heart attack, and I was going almost daily to my parents' house where he was ensconced, Dr. Gudauskas stopping in daily. Ed would meet me there after school and we would often have dinner with them, glimpsing that we had to seize the day with my father.

But he was recovering well, and we felt quite content to encourage Ed's mother to take her first trip to Ireland. After our visit and discovery of "lost" O'Donnell relatives, she had gotten very interested, and they had written her warmly suggesting a visit. So we sent her off that June on what would be her first of many trips to Ireland and the beginning of a close relationship with the Ryan-Browne family which is flowering even in the present day.

In July, just after our first anniversary, I had had a pregnancy test which turned out negative. Having the non-scientist's faith in a not-very-scientific measurement, I panicked. Ed was going to visit the doctor who had operated on his knee before marriage and mentioned it. Dr. Fischer was obviously surprised that we would put faith in such a primitive measurement as were rabbit tests, and I gratefully accepted his referral to a gynecologist-obstetrician whom I visited the very next week. Dr. Lane kindly explained the unreliability of such tests, examined me, and said, "Since you have had this test, I will tell you that you probably are pregnant. If you hadn't had it, I would say it's definite." Eight months later, Mary Kate was born. We were no longer a couple, but a family.

XXVIII
Mary Kate

When we joyfully found out that we were expecting Mary Kate, I thought of the fact that, God-willing, I would be very pregnant by the end of January, which was when the semester at Loyola ended. I wanted to teach the first semester and called John Gerrietts, the bachelor chairman, just to clear the matter. He was quite surprised, maybe even shocked in 1959, and said he would have to "check with the administration." When one considers all the time and attention given today to prevent discrimination against young women who want to have both career and family, we realize just how many light years we have progressed since then. Fortunately for me, a rather liberal dean of the graduate school, Father Stewart E. Dollard, whom I had known for years, thought it was a "delightful idea" to have a pregnant woman teaching at Loyola. So I was home free.

The winter of '59–'60 was a rough one, with a great deal of ice and snow, and we had a hard time keeping the walks clear. I had always loved to shovel snow and insisted on claiming that job, but now pregnant, I was forbidden to do so. Ed's knee, so recently and precariously repaired, prevented him from shoveling, so my father sent out two fellows to clean our walk who had come into Chicago Granitine looking for work. I remember seeing them standing in our basement at Maplewood Ave. and wondering how recently they had exchanged prison garb for the dungarees they now wore. To my father, this was a reprise of his 1930s experience of finding a man who had just come out of the unemployment line and offering him work.

As March, the due date, approached, I would go to the doctor each week and Ed would meet me after his classes, in the Marshall Field's waiting room on the third floor. We would go to the seventh floor, have coffee at the buffet, and fortify ourselves against a snowy weekend with a coffee cake from the bakery there. I remember how shocked

I was, years later when I came to Marshall Field's third floor, only to find the waiting room gone, turned into an ice cream parlor which yielded revenue for the store. I have often wondered if that was when people who had access to suburban shopping malls decided to stop going downtown. Why, there even had been a message book one could write in. There you said something like, "Kevin, I have gone to the toy department. Meet me there—3:20 p.m.—Mom."

We wondered if the baby would come in the midst of a snow storm, and when I began to feel a few pains about midnight on March 9, we called Dr. Lane who was rather nondirective, saying that it might be the real thing and then again it might not. We chose the latter, misinterpreting his message and turned over in bed until about 2:00 a.m. when the signs were unmistakable. We called Garden Cab, and the poor driver almost lost his dinner when he found out he would be driving a woman in labor down the Outer Drive on a snowy night. When we arrived and got into the elevator, there were a number of hospital workers on it, but the operator took one look at me and sped to maternity. Dr. Lane was waiting, a little annoyed that we hadn't come earlier, as he evidently had done. When Mary Kate was finally born at 7:55 a.m. on March 10, Ed was in time to catch my father and mother before Dad left for work. Ed's mom was duly informed and we all rejoiced over our most-welcome daughter. We had played our cards close to the chest about names, joking that it would be Cunegunda if the new member of the family was a girl. I remember receiving a telegram from Frank and Betty Riley in San Antonio which read "Glory be to St. Cunegunda for Mary Kate."

My roommate was a Jewish woman who had just had a boy after two girls, and I learned quite a bit about orthodox circumcision from her. The Rabbi who would perform the surgery had to be licensed and could not travel on the Sabbath. Consequently, he had to be housed at a local hotel, near enough for him to be available without such traveling on the first day that it was ritualistically appropriate. It was all very interesting to this new mother, and I gratefully got a lot of realistic advice from this mother of three.

We were all set to go home on March 16, but heavy snow fell on the night of the Ides of March. My father's voice on the phone bore the bad news. "Reconcile yourself to another day in the hospital—

the weather is too bad." Since he was the chauffeur, I grudgingly assented. How different from the "option" available to a young mother in this era of managed care. So that is how the Kearneys happened to be going home for the first time on St. Patrick's Day, 1960, where Grandmother Mary had made sure the crib and bath table were prepared while Grandma Genevieve held forth with the roast beef in the kitchen. We were on our own but with experienced grandmas close at hand. Two and a half weeks later Mary Kate was baptized with Pat and Pat Grogan as her godparents. We had begun our mission of parenthood.

XXIX
Dad's Death

At Mary Kate's christening, my dad told the Pats and us that he was declaring a dividend in honor of Mary Kate's birth and each of us would get a new car. It was so like his philosophy of gift giving. People should receive what they really need and want, but not when they would expect it. We had been driving the 1951 Plymouth which I had before we were married, and the heater no longer worked. The previous winter, we had gone to Ray and Mary Simon's house, after seeing them at Bea Cunningham's wedding, and I remember that we were almost frozen when we got to their North Sheridan Road apartment on a wintery Saturday. Now, with a baby, having no heater could be a real problem, so his offer was an unexpected bonus at this time of increased family expense. My brother, too, was still in the struggling years of his certified public accounting career, so the news of a new car was most welcome. Pat was to get the new car my father promised, but when my father died so soon after this announcement, we took over his automobile since my mother had never driven in Chicago. The money which Dad had so thoughtfully put aside for his gift we used for other needs.

As the first weeks of our new daughter's life progressed, my mother reported that Dad was suffering from a severe cold. As he was always prone to bronchial problems, we did not take it too seriously, so the call from my mother on April 6 was a shock. She said that Dr. Gudauskas had diagnosed his malady as viral pneumonia, and his breathing was labored. As I consider the matter now, I wonder if immediate hospitalization with assistance to his respiration might have saved his life. He had always dreaded hospitals and had battled both of his heart attacks without ever leaving his home and he refused to do it now. It was no time to oppose a sick man.

I called Mrs. Atchley, the nice neighbor to the south, and she stayed with Mary Kate while Ed's mother came in a cab. When we got to

Green Street, my mother's and brother's faces told the story. Dad was struggling for breath. Dr. Gudauskas and one of the priests from St. Leo came in. Within a couple of hours, he was gone. The man who had been my hero, the "greatest man in the world" as he had taught me to say, the man who had loved me and laughed with me, told me when I got "100" on a paper in first grade that he always got a hundred and ten, teased me out of heartbreak after broken romances, charmed my teachers and friends, and won the heart and admiration of my husband, was gone.

Just what he was to many others I was to learn during the days of the wake and funeral. When we said the Rosary together, Dad always had added an "Our Father" and "Hail Mary" for our "friends, relatives, and benefactors." We often asked who the last-mentioned were, and he would smile mysteriously and say, "You never know who has helped you along the way . . . ." To this day when we say grace on holidays and at family dinners, we always add an invocation for "friends, relatives, and benefactors." That he was one of the last-mentioned, for many people, I discovered during his wake when people whose names I never knew came with stories of how he had helped them out just at the point in their lives when they really needed it— in the form of a job, a stake for some training, a down-payment, or just a few bucks to "carry you through." Robert Stephen Grogan had been born in the era of self-made men. He knew that his own hard work and perseverance had propelled him, but he knew also that the grace of God and the blessing of St. Patrick along with a bit of Irish luck and the help of "benefactors" had sustained him, and he was bound and determined that we would do the same for others since his efforts had borne such fruit.

I was devastated by the loss, and even more by the fact that my children, month-old Mary Kate and future hoped-for children, would never know him. My husband Ed promised me, as I wept beside him in bed that night, that this would never happen. And it has not. Mary Kate, Edmund Martin, John Grogan, Joseph Dinneen, and Robert Augustine have all been made to feel they knew this man and that each one has something of him within himself. Robert Grogan lives in the quick laugh and dramatic presence of Mary Kate, in Edmund's walk and John's outrageous humor, in Joseph's compassion, and in Robert's way with words. At least once a month I look at Ed when one of them comes out with something that smacks of my father or when one of them says something like "your friends need no explanations; your enemies won't believe them anyway." Then I know we succeeded in our project of keeping R.S. alive.

XXX
Early Years of Parenting and Edmund

We have often said that we didn't fully appreciate the baby Mary Kate until we had Edmund, but we really did. Our pediatrician, Dr. Fleming, was not the easiest person to talk to, and heaven knows, I needed help with my first baby. He had the theory that babies should adjust to the world and its demands, not vice versa. Consequently, when even a new baby woke up at night, one should check her condition, possibly change the diapers, and make her wait for the next feeding time. After one night of that, fortunately Ed's common sense, or need for sleep when he had eight o'clock classes, enabled us to reject that counsel, and we found that with one two o'clock feeding she was perfect. Of course we didn't bother to inform Dr. Fleming about that so he continued on his course without feedback from mothers who were, I suspect, scared to death of him.

I know that I was, and I often turned to Mr. George O'Brien, pharmacist, for advice. I remember, one time, Mary Kate had been playing with a Raggedy Ann doll in her playpen which was in a dining room "L" next to the kitchen. When I went to pick her up, her whole face was covered with red, from Raggedy's hair which, of course, she had been chewing on. I ran to the phone to tell Mr. O'Brien and was reassured by his knowledge that toxic materials had been outlawed for some time in children's toys.

My mother would come out at least one day a week, driven by my Uncle Joe on his barbers' day off, and she would be laden with groceries she had just included in her order from Auburn Foods and Liquor. Bob the butcher and my mother were close confederates in keeping us well-supplied and when she was there I could run out for necessary errands. Ed's mother would stay a few days when she came, so we had a lot of free, loving baby-sitting which we didn't use as fruitfully as we could have.

Ed was getting a ride home from school with Dixie Jordan, a woman in her thirties with a four-year-old son whose husband was very ill, and her mode of talk to a young baby and the response that she got taught me a lot. She would often stop in and I would be amazed at how our seemingly contented baby would swing into responsive mode when Dixie bent her head close over the playpen and talked.

Then came spring break in May. I would bring Mary Kate into the bedroom, plop her next to her reading father, and run to the basement to wash diapers. When I would come up, I could hear the two of them laughing, and the alternation of his deep voice and her coos and giggles would convince me that these two were having a conversation. I know they bonded during that period. I recently read that babies learn during those first months the rubrics of human conversation in what they hear, and our little girl was ready for it. I often wonder if the stage for her early precocity wasn't set in those father-daughter sessions.

She and I began a regime of walks even in cold weather and we could be glimpsed almost any morning or afternoon trekking the sidewalks of the Beverly Woods area between 115th and 119th, from Western to the railroad tracks. Ed was so protective of her that I remember one of my friends from a club to which I belonged stopping in with a gift and her four-year-old daughter who had recently had a cold. As she entered, I heard her tell this to Ed and was horrified to hear him say, "You won't mind if we don't show you the baby, we don't want her to get sick."

Our mothers called the baby the Val-lo-wil chicken, an allusion to the promoter of an almost all-white-meat chicken who claimed that his fowl never touched the ground. Ed was always there with a blanket when I was ready to put her on the floor, and I began to wonder if he could ever relax and enjoy this baby we had wanted so much. He did, of course, when she was joined by her brother Edmund, sixteen months later.

On New Year's Day of 1961, we took our mothers out to dinner at Cavallini's and told them that we were expecting a second baby. They were as happy as we were, and soon we found out that Pat and Pat, my brother and his wife, were expecting a baby right around the same time. Mark Grogan and Edmund Kearney were born just six days apart in July 1961. Our family was expanding.

When I went to the doctor in late July, he told me that the baby was in the right position for delivery and jokingly added, "If you have any pains on the way home, you'd better come back." The car was parked near 63rd and Loomis, and I had taken the Englewood "L" down to Dr. Lane's office next to Wesley Memorial Hospital. I was all the way to 43rd St. on the way home when I convinced myself that I was in labor, disembarked, crossed over the bridge across the tracks, and returned. I need not have hurried because Edmund wasn't born until well into the night, on July 22, 1961, but it gave him a chance to say, in later years, "My father made my mother take the L to have me."

The car, of course, was still at 63rd, so Ed asked Dr. Chada's son, Joe, to pick it up there. Joe was one of Ed's students and became a good friend. After all, he was an accessory to the fact.

We came home from the hospital in late July driven by Pastor Timmerman and Marc Coine, two of Ed's friends from Chicago Teachers College, who told us that a terrible murder had just taken place on the North Shore. Pastor Timmerman, a Lutheran minister, to lighten the atmosphere said that he was glad to hear that his Catholic friends were choosing an appropriate middle name—Martin. Mary Kate, aged sixteen months, now had a brother who would soon become her playmate and friend—Edmund Martin Kearney.

But once home with our little family, he did not seem to be settling in. The baby, Edmund, lost much of the formula I was feeding him and seemed terribly distressed after feedings. Only walking back and forth with him sometimes settled him down. Ed's mother came to stay with us and she and I would take turns at night going back and forth with him after the two o'clock feeding. She hadn't walked without a cane in years, but she managed to do so with her grandson. We sent Ed to sleep in the other bedroom for he had to be up and out for the eight o'clock class.

Either I was not telling Dr. Fleming how bad it was, or he wasn't hearing me, for I remember an incident which we laughed over later, but was all too real at the time. Mom Kearney had gone back to her

30 ~ Early Years of Parenting & Edmund

apartment, but would call daily to see how her grandson was doing. One day I told her that I thought he looked scrawny, sort of like a picked chicken. That evening, when she went to her refrigerator and saw the chicken the Lavezzis had purchased for her in their weekend shopping, she was unable to prepare and eat it. It looked too much like my description of Edmund.

Finally, at nine weeks, we appealed to Dr. John L. Reichert, the pediatrician at Wesley Memorial Hospital where Edmund had been born. Well known and respected, he was at that time the president of the Board of Education. We made the trip to Howard Street on the border between Evanston and Chicago, where his office was located. He took one look at our nine-week old son who had weighed 7 pounds 11 ounces at birth and now weighed only 9 pounds and exclaimed, "Good heavens, this baby is suffering from malnutrition; he may have to be hospitalized." I was shocked.

After careful questioning and refusing all phone calls that would distract him from our little boy, he addressed us seriously, "There is one thing we might try. Both your nursing and the formula are based on milk. There is just a chance that he is allergic to milk. We'll start him on soybean formula, but if he doesn't start to gain immediately, then he'll have to go to the hospital."

We said our prayers, bought the soyalac, and took our little boy home. He stopped spitting up his milk, and we could see him begin to thrive visibly. Each month Ed and I or my mother and I would go to Howard Street, holding Baby Edmund as was customary in those days before infant security seats. We remember one blindingly snowy night when we were ticketed by a sour-faced policeman, who glanced at the struggling mother, trying to control her car against traffic and weather, and the father holding his baby son. When the Summerdale police scandal erupted a short time later, we hoped that he was one of those brought down. Technically, we deserved the ticket for an illegal left turn, but we thought that those policemen should have been employing their efforts elsewhere where they were more needed.

At the end of Edmund's first year, he was a chubby, healthy baby and was soon able to drink regular milk. Dr. Reichert told us, "I'm going to send you to a doctor you won't have trouble talking to." He recommended Ralph Spaeth who took care of all our children from that day on and remains our dear friend. When Dr. Reichert died of a heart attack while alone in his office one Saturday afternoon a couple of years later, we mourned the passing of the man who had said that day, "I don't want to talk to anybody. The only important thing to me is this baby."

Dr. Reichert had told us to keep the baby almost upright after feedings, so a familiar sight at our dinner table was Mary Kate in her high chair, Ed and I at each end, and Baby Edmund propped in his infant seat as the centerpiece. When each of his three younger brothers was born and had a little trouble with digestion, I quickly turned to the foul-smelling soybean mixture as our answer.

XXXI
Transitions

Once we got Edmund on his way into a healthy little boyhood, Ed reminded me that I hadn't taught on Saturday since Edmund was born, and it was now November. So when they called from Loyola to see if I would be back to my Saturday teaching, second semester, Ed encouraged me to say "yes." My mother was shocked, as I think his mother was. He argued that I needed the stimulus with one baby not yet two years old and the other a few months. Given Edmund's problem with eating, I was quite uneasy. My mother offered to come out on Saturday, and Mrs. Thelen said she would do it when my mother couldn't.

Helen Thelen was a woman who had teenage children and a special way with little ones. She came to help one day a week when I was expecting Edmund, and what a treasure she was. After a day of heavy cleaning when she was ready to leave, and little Mary Kate wanted to have a tea party, she would take off her coat, and enter into the spirit of the act, drinking the imaginary tea which the dramatic two-year old would pour.

During the week on days Helen was at our house she would also keep up a steady stream of conversation with the children as she worked. After we all had lunch together, Edmund in the center of the table in his infant seat, I was free to go to Carson's at the nearby Evergreen Plaza to have my hair done. I think I especially appreciated the luxury afforded me because I had been so confined with Edmund. With this resourceful experienced mother of four, I was completely confident that all crises would be handled, probably better than I could have managed them.

A bonus of her being at our house on Thursdays was that we could renew our subscription to the Goodman Theatre. I would pick Ed up at Chicago Teachers College every sixth Thursday and we would proceed downtown, leaving time for a relaxing dinner at the Berghoff, and still be there for the 7:30 Goodman curtain. Indeed, there was life after children.

As the year progressed, it became increasingly evident that we had outgrown our house. After dinner and the kids' bedtime each night, Ed would go into the study to do some work, pay some bills, or prepare his classes. Mary Kate had been such a peaceful baby, sleeping through the night, that we assumed Edmund would be the same, once his digestive problems were solved. But after Ed would be in there for a half hour or so, he would emerge, exclaiming, "I can't work in there with his beady little eyes looking at me over the bumper." We had put Edmund in the study because of his frequent and often-noisy feedings, thinking it could serve a dual purpose. We were very wrong.

I contacted Sears Roebuck in hopes they could suggest a convenient way to expand our three-bedroom, one-bath house. So many random events affect the decisions of our lives. The man they sent out was singularly pessimistic. It would be more than difficult, he asserted, to do this on our thirty-five-foot lot, with the bedrooms on the back and the bathroom in the center of the house. The position of these bedrooms was a real problem too, I thought, for I could picture myself trying to see my toddlers playing in the yard while I was working in the centrally located kitchen, and it seemed impossible. I remembered, too, my father's words when we were married and I questioned certain features of the Maplewood house. He said, "When your needs are different, buy another house."

We began to look in earnest and enlisted the help of a wonderfully sympathetic realtor who was the senior salesman for Mulholland Real Estate, a firm well established in Beverly and whose founder, Clem Mulholland, was the father of one of my Longwood classmates. We knew we would have to go into an older home to get the space we needed within a reasonable price range, and I had certain prejudices based upon some small bungalows I had known with enough rooms but cramped dimensions. I also had recollections of my father's calling a home with all the bedrooms upstairs "woman killers." So Mr. John Craven had a real job fulfilling my conditions, and he regretfully said, after one of my speeches, that it was too bad he couldn't show us "the most beautiful bungalow in Beverly."

That phrase haunted us, and one day, after a fruitless visit to yet another house, I called him—would he show us that bungalow? It must have been late April on an unusually warm, sunny day because all the French windows were open in the bay opening off the dining room at Oakley Avenue as one of the two daughters of the family sat there with a huge collie dog at her feet. The windows all had gold awnings, the proportions of the living and dining rooms were more than generous, and there was a grassed-in lot next door, the same width as the one the house was built on—sixty feet. It was stunning.

We had hopes of having more children and were disappointed when I had a miscarriage later that month. We temporarily put aside plans for buying a house. Suddenly, at the end of spring (about mid-May) when I was feeling better, I remembered the scene of the girl and the collie dog and the open French windows. I told Ed of my feelings that night, and next morning I called Mr. Craven at home, holding my breath lest it was already sold. It was not and he suggested we make another visit, this time bringing our mothers if we wished. Smart man! That night, with Mary Kearney and Genevieve Grogan along, we paid another and more serious visit. Our mothers liked the house, and we decided to make an offer. It was accepted, and we were, nominally at least, the owners of two houses.

That wasn't a situation we hoped would continue very long. We showed our first house a few Sundays without any success and, finally, in early August we moved to our larger and older house in the heart of Beverly, hoping that with our other house empty, just the right buyer would come along. It took a long time for that to happen, but we honestly never lost any sleep over it. That may have been a reflection of our naiveté, but it served us well. We had gotten to know a number of realtors in the months while we were looking. Some of them were old friends like Frank Reynolds or new friends like John Craven, but they and a few others whom we knew were given keys and were then able to bring people through the empty house.

One of them, Mr. Sam Dunne, provided a prospect, and this seasoned older man patiently guided us through the intricate dance, alternately luring and limiting a prospective buyer, not insulting him by having the price too high and seemingly inflexible, but not opening the door to an extremely low bid either. Knowing as little as we did about the process, we trusted his judgment, and he served us well. Finally, we sold our Maplewood Avenue house in November and settled ourselves comfortably into what we hoped would be a long tenure in our second home. It has been a long and happy one.

XXXII
Oakley House, John's Arrival, and the Loss of a Mother

As we became more accustomed to our "new" older house on Oakley Avenue, we also became aware of some things which needed alteration. The two daughters of the previous owners had carpeted the three-quarters bathroom, formerly a pantry, in a pink fluffy bath rug which my mother said she could not imagine with two toddlers. Could she give us a tile floor as part of the housewarming? She certainly could, we answered with alacrity.

Also, Edmund, at thirteen months, was crawling around everywhere and invariably came up with dirty hands and knees. When we called Service Master to give us an estimate on cleaning the rug in the living room which was approximately twenty by thirty with a dining room and bay of almost the same size, they told me they had just cleaned the carpeting before the house was sold. "It's so deep, lady, that if you go any more than one-third down, you get mildew." So much for clean knees! We settled down and it served us for over thirty years when it was suddenly no longer thick.

My brother, customarily sardonic, on a visit sat at one end of our very wide living room and suggested that we could put the coffin at one side and line up all the mourners' chairs on the other. Obviously, it was a house that needed some artistry. And we needed help! Down to John A. Colby we trotted and there a designer made a plot of our floor plan, suggesting two groupings of furniture and projecting a more attractive image, we thought, of our very large rooms with 1920s French leaded-glass windows throughout.

This large bungalow, built by Mr. O'Leary in the 1920s before the stock market crash brought a hiatus to such activities, was a challenge. That my initial love affair with it, begun that sunny afternoon when the daughter of the former owner sat in the bay off the dining room, has never grown cold is a testament to its good lines and lasting appeal. It is yellow brick with large gold awnings, a look which we lost when those awnings wore out. Ed replaced them as a surprise for me a few years ago, and the visage I remembered was essentially restored.

We had hoped for a larger family, and when another miscarriage occurred before the end of our first year in the house, we were discouraged. When I became pregnant again, Pope John XXIII was on the papal throne "opening the windows" of the church, and he had recently been diagnosed as terminally ill with cancer. I prayed that, if he died, his intercession would bring us a third child. Dr. Lane had told me there was no reason to be concerned for our expected child, but my two miscarriages had rocked my confidence. When John Grogan Kearney was born on my mother's birthday in 1963, October 11, we breathed signs of relief and prayers of thanksgiving. He was named for Ed's deceased father, John, and for Pope John XXIII. When I was in labor, Dr. Lane jokingly asked if I was now convinced that I would not miscarry at three months. This baby, so welcome, would change our lives possibly more even than his older brother and sister had.

When we bought the house, the family living there owned the lot to the south and kept it grassed in like a park. It was a tempting offer when they said they had left it that way until the new owners had an opportunity to purchase it along with the house. But it was out of the question for us, a young couple starting out, to take that on. Perhaps, we calculated, it would not be sold right away and we could ultimately purchase it. Within the week, it was sold to Mr. Julius Kemmler, a local commercial contractor who built the house now owned by Gaudy Paris, our good friend. The Kemmlers were an older couple whose three children were grown and whose grandchildren, visiting regularly, played with our children. While we regretted the loss of the grassed-in lot, the Kemmlers and later the Paris family became our good friends. Mr. Kemmler had a few unusual ideas like having a fountain in the middle of the back yard which the Paris family ultimately had to remove.

On the other side of our house lived a large family who seemingly should have had a great deal in common with us—religion, nationality, and educational level. However, the constant problems which their remarks and physical interference brought made our enjoyment of our new home less than complete. Our driveways were immediately adjacent, which could provide a problem without mutual respect and consideration practiced on both families' parts. Since there was none of that or even consciousness of its need on their part, there was a constant feeling of tension. In order to minimize contact, we had our little ones take bikes and wagons down the other side of the house, rather than the more natural driveway side. One time when my mother inquired why this was being done, little Edmund sweetly looked at her and answered, "Why Gwamma, they are barbarians." (Pronounced bah-bawians.) Several times during the '60s and '70s, we thought of moving because of the neighbors on that side, but could never bring ourselves to give up our house which we loved.

Eventually they moved and were replaced by more convivial neighbors. But this experience taught me that double driveways with cars parked right next to one another almost always invite conflict if there is any lack of good feeling.

Our house, built in 1928, was in the center of what had been three lots. The driveway and the garage would more properly have been placed on the other side of the lot. The plumbing contractor for the city, Mr. O'Leary, had perhaps envisioned that his larger yellow bungalow might permanently sit in the middle of his three lots. As it turned out, one lot to the north was sold and built on immediately after World War II (1947), and the other to the south remained grassed in until we bought O'Leary's house and indicated that we had no interest in purchasing it.

Each night when we would put Edmund and Mary Kate to bed in the two adjoining bedrooms, we would close the doors between until we went to bed a few hours later. Each night I would smell gas in Baby Edmund's room and worry about it until Ed checked on it. By the time he got there the odor would have dissipated and we could go to bed with ease. One Saturday night Ed's mother went to the bathroom next door and announced that she would open the bedroom door. Immediately, she called out that there was a distinct aroma of gas there. We notified the gas company who worked all night and next day to tear up the driveway and cut off the leak. We thanked God that the leak was on the gas company's side of the line.

Elsewhere in the house, the little sun porch back of the kitchen was useless to us for much of the year. It was a heat trap in summer and a place only to keep boots and sleds in the winter, and we began looking into altering it. A young carpenter who had been trained when he was temporarily a member of a religious brotherhood took on the job. We didn't yet know Pat King, our wonderful friend and master carpenter, or perhaps we would have added the family room then as we did a few years later. We made the addition into a breakfast room, one step down from our kitchen. But we were foolish enough to leave the concrete floor under the tile we put down. This saved money, but made the floor quite hard. It was wonderful to have a real back door finally, and we used that breakfast room for playpens, tables, and all the overflow from our growing family. The house we had bought had lots of formal space in the front but not much play area. Gradually, our house was becoming more of the home we have today. Ed says that was his mistake—implementing my ideas. More than thirty years later we are still here and I, at least, am still loving it.

John was a far more active baby than either Mary Kate or Edmund had been. He slept little but advanced normally, walking at an earlier age than anyone else. What amazed us was that he started to talk before he ever walked and long sentences filled with logical but ungrammatical verbs issued forth. He also proved to have an ear for the inappropriate. One morning a couple of years later, I decided to attend a weekday Mass at St. Barnabas, our parish church. An old-fashioned red brick structure, it had many steps up to the door. By that time, I had another baby, Joseph, in my arms and almost two-year-old John felt that I was dragging him along so that I would get in before communion. Always explosive and with a voice that rang out loud and clear, he yelled, "I hate you, damn it anyway." All the white-haired St. Barnabas matrons, as with a single movement, turned their heads to see from whence the eruption came and beheld a pint-size prophet standing in the middle aisle with a woman, babe in arms, stopped dead in her tracks. That was not the last time I would be embarrassed by John's tongue, because small as he was, his voice sounded like that of a much older child. In a supermarket, he would comment on the products, the people, and his mother in such a way that brought entertainment and embarrassment. Smaller of stature than Edmund, he was quick as lightning and able to extricate himself from almost any restraint. Little wonder that I yearned for the day that he could go off to Beverly Community Nursery School a couple of mornings each week.

Meanwhile, my mother had had a recurrence of a cancerous condition she had dealt with before and faced surgery. Her heart and circulatory system were impaired and she entered the hospital in July, just after Edmund's fourth birthday, for treatment to improve this condition. Within the preceding weeks, she had made a will and taken care of a number of personal obligations that she had had in mind. Since my father's death five years earlier, she had spent her time and money giving of herself to family and friends. I remember taking Edmund to the hospital where she was getting the presurgical treatment, and she was able to come to a sun room to visit with him. He had always had a special place in her heart, having spent a lot of time at Green Street while his older sister, easier to care for, had more often been at Grandma Kearney's. He remembers that visit well, and it was to be his last, for a few weeks later she died after surgery, her heart not able to handle the shock. My mother was a great lady and I feel that she is still watching over us up there. When it initially seemed that Edmund's baby, Brendan Anthony, might have some health problems, I regularly asked her intercession.

After her death, I prayed for another child and feel she was instrumental in sending Robert Augustine into our lives on September 12, 1966. It was high time we named one of our sons after my father, and Ed felt that Augustine was a saint and philosopher who was the greatest figure of the early church. As a little boy, Rob thought the moniker Augustine rather burdensome, but as a grown man he wears it proudly. As for the Robert, he is the perfect bearer of my sharp, funny, slightly outrageous father's psyche. We think we have succeeded in keeping my parents alive through stories about them, and now we have a real live Robert who truly deserves the name.

XXXIII
Joseph

Our joy knew no bounds when, after all our worry about John's safe delivery, we found ourselves expecting again in the late spring of 1964. John kept us hopping to stay a jump ahead of him. For instance, I went to the front door to get mail one day leaving him in a little infant seat in the kitchen, only to return less than a minute later to find him turned upside down on the floor. This child, we knew, was different.

One day when he was about six weeks old, I was changing him on a pad on the kitchen table, cocking one ear to the television set for "As the World Turns." Suddenly the program was interrupted with a news flash that there had been a shooting in Dallas, and it was thought that the president was injured. Shocked, I watched for Ed to come home from school, and within a short time we knew that Kennedy had been killed. Images of Jacqueline Kennedy, strong in her grief, and of a solemn-faced Lyndon Johnson being sworn in aboard Air Force One were everywhere.

One of the nuns at St. Xavier told me that Mrs. Kennedy had contacted the convent in Washington where the Sisters of Mercy were providing religious instruction for little Caroline Kennedy to invite them for a semi-private attendance at President Kennedy's wake in Washington. We all marveled at her composure and grasp of details, each one of us wondering how she would react under similar circumstances.

Ed and I talked long and hard about our private grief at the loss of this young president who seemed to offer such hope to America. At the very least, such an event brought everyone face-to-face with one's own mortality and gave us the accompanying spur to cherish our loved ones and our moments together.

As the autumn when John was a year old progressed, and Joseph's growing self within me became a more noticeable presence, we talked

33 — Joseph

of this impending delivery, expecting it in early 1965. But three days after Christmas when I visited Dr. Lane for my regular check-up, he found that I was dilating and thus open up to infection. He suggested that I enter the hospital and Ed came down to be with me. Joseph was born that night and Ed found himself with a new income tax deduction, in 1964 rather than 1965. The closeness to Christmas and the presence of the nativity scenes everywhere prompted us to choose the name Joseph. He was small, six pounds, five ounces, but beautiful.

One day while I was still in the hospital, he gave us a scare. Babies were brought to mothers for every feeding at the then Wesley Memorial Hospital, and Joseph's breathing seemed labored. Leona Reynolds was visiting that day so we went down the hall to the nursery afterwards to see how he was doing. He seemed very uncomfortable so I asked that he be seen by the hospital's pediatrician immediately. To my shock they answered that there was no one in the building, but they would send up to Children's Memorial. Meanwhile, while we waited, the baby was left with me. My roommate had gone home and I was left alone with this new person who was so precious to us. I took him into the bathroom, and remembering from my early catechism that it was the intent that mattered, I poured water over his head and baptized him. A few minutes later the pediatrician arrived, told me it was newborn mucous in his nose, and sucked it out with a syringe. They sent me home a couple of days later with a syringe for future emergencies, of which, fortunately, there were none.

We had already determined that we were going to ask Jack and Mary Ellen Clark to be Joseph's godparents, and when Ed and they went over to St. Barnabas to arrange for recording the baptism, they said they would repeat the whole thing. So the solemnization of the baptism may have taken place at St. Barnabas, but we know when Joseph was baptized. The arrival of Joseph Dinneen Kearney to our family circle was indeed a momentous event. Dinneen was Ed's mother's maiden name and we continued our tradition begun with John Grogan.

Joseph turned out to have curls when his hair grew in and a more angelic-looking baby could not be found. While John had been distinguished by his ability to get in and out of things and his string of seasoned invective always quite decipherable by anyone within a half-block, Joseph was the one who could remove the little screw and make the whole toy fall apart. More and more I would be asked by Mary Kate and Edmund to "put this up in your precious cabinet," a shelf I kept in the kitchen for things that they didn't want broken by Joseph.

One cold Easter we were at my brother's for dinner, and Susan, my oldest niece, was zipping cherubic Joseph into his snow suit. When she finished tussling with him, she grinningly said, "He may look like Jesus, but he ain't no Jesus." It is a remark remembered.

Joseph was trying to say things, but we couldn't understand him. I remembered Sister Antonine, the speech teacher at St. Xavier College where I taught for two years before marriage. A visit to her confirmed his lazy tongue and we started in on a couple of years of twice-weekly visits to her speech clinic. I would drop him off and either go to the snack bar or stay over to the side correcting papers while the five or six children, mainly boys, had their class. When I would pick him up at the end of the period, Sr. Antonine often said, "Everybody did fine, but Joe was the best." I chalked it up to familiarity with me as a former colleague and was surprised when she called me aside soon after he was four to say, "Is there any place where you can get him into school next year before he is five? He is a very bright child and won't practice these tongue exercises until he wants people to understand his thoughts. He needs real school!"

So that is how Joseph ended up at Morgan Park Academy at four years and eight months. I thought of all that when I saw him mount the steps to the pulpit of Holy Name Cathedral as the valedictorian of his St. Ignatius College Prep class many years later, and I thanked God for people like Sister Antonine who recognized in this angelic lisper a potential lawyer.

XXXIV
THE 1960S: A FAMILY A' BUILDING

Our children's early years went by rapidly but certain images leap out. Mary Kate was the little girl who always wanted to hear the next chapter. With three little boys and then four, I didn't have time to read all the stories which would bring magic to her life, and we had long ago decided that we would use television only as an occasional selected treat. Her delight at the spoken word was obvious as far back as crib time when Ed read from the *Oxford Dictionary of Nursery Rhymes*. Her favorite was "Here comes a candle to light you to bed, Here comes a chopper to chop off your head." Edmund responded to "I see the moon, and the moon sees me; God bless the priest that christened me."

Gradually an idea began to form in my mind. The public school nearby was rigid in its starting-age requirements, and I suspected the Catholic school might be equally inflexible. We had been going to the Cenacle Convent, the old Walgreen Mansion at 116th and Longwood Drive, one morning a week for pre-school religious instruction. Lila, our lovely ironing lady, would come to stay with the little ones and as we went there, we would pass Morgan Park Military Academy, an impressive structure on 111th with several buildings and a great deal of wooded land stretching almost to 115th Street.

Through the years, even in my childhood, one would see the uniformed boys from the military academy on outings with parents or a chaperon. I had heard that in the '60s, as military academies were less popular, there was a movement to open the school to girls. So I called, and could hardly believe the voice that answered. "Oh yes, we aren't a military academy any longer. We have been adding grades downward each year. Next year we plan to have a first grade and kindergarten. But the kindergartners have to be ready to learn to read because they will be right in with the first graders." It sounded like a description of paradise for Mary Kate. Ed and I talked it over and decided our oldest child needed some stimulation. We would see if she qualified. Mary Kate had had her fourth birthday in March. Saturdays were my "day out" when I taught at Loyola and sometimes met a friend for lunch, and either my mother or Mrs. Thelen was there to help with the children on Saturday. So Ed took Mary Kate over to the 111th Street campus of Morgan Park Academy to be tested. Whatever reading readiness test they gave her, she passed easily. The teacher giving the test added almost as an afterthought, "Before she starts, though, maybe you could teach her how to button her coat." With that, our decision was made, but our mothers were harder to convince. Without their saying so, we could see that they thought we were pushing our first child. Somehow we knew she was ready, and when she happily went off on the school bus that beautiful September morning, never looking back to wave, we were sure of it.

We had kept the children away from large gatherings full of germs for the most part, so Mary Kate picked up everything that fall, even landing in the hospital to prevent what Dr. Spaeth feared might become dehydration after repeated vomiting. But she emerged from that, returning eagerly to school. The magic had begun to happen. She was learning to read, and the mysterious black marks on paper were turning into stories. Another reader was born. I don't know if she was able to read her beloved Bobbsey Twins immediately, but I remember that it did not take long.

When she entered first grade the next September, and would be gone the whole day, we thought that Edmund, her pal, would miss her greatly. He was three, and I had heard good things about Beverly Community Nursery School, housed in a Unitarian Church at 103rd and Longwood Drive. I called up to inquire about it and carefully couched my questions with a condition: "You don't teach them any religion, do you?" I didn't want my little Catholic to turn into a Unitarian. The merry laugh reassured me. "We wouldn't exist if it were not for the Catholics of Beverly, Mrs. Kearney." The answer revealed how things had changed. Beverly had always been a securely WASP area, to the extent that there was great objection to the building of St. Barnabas some years before. Many of the residents felt that the Catholics were amply taken care of, with St. Margaret at 99th and Throop, and they were not that anxious to have more of "those people" (Catholics) in their pristine neighborhood. But things had changed since then.

Since I had Lila to iron on Tuesdays and Mrs. Thelen on Thursdays, I was free to take Edmund to nursery school, and it was often a time-consuming job. When I took him there, Edmund would fuss for quite a while, agreeing to stay only because I was sitting over to the side. Finally after I saw that he had been sufficiently engaged by Mrs. Knott and Mrs. Lee, the very capable teachers, I could blow him a kiss and leave. As I would pull out of the parking lot of this stately edifice which an Irishman had built on the model of a particular Irish castle, I would wonder every time if I was doing the right thing. Edmund was very attached to me, and I knew that I would have little hope of sending him happily off to kindergarten in two years if he did not get used to going off to school a couple of days per week. A recent discussion with Edmund about why we sent him off to nursery school twice weekly has shown me that he still remembers it as a trauma. I think I know a lot more about early childhood development now than I did then and would probably keep him home for those two years. But one's parenting with older children is often a combination of one's own instinct, upbringing, and things that one has read, so we did our best with our number 1 son. He was a sweet and serious child who had some memorable lines like the one to my mother about the "Bahbawians" next door.

One night in December of 1964, just before Joseph was born, we were going to a Chicago Teachers College affair and I was feeling that even my maternity clothes felt very tight. I was in the kitchen just before we left and couldn't reach over my burgeoning stomach to put something in the dishwasher. I said, "Oh I'm as big as a house!" and three-year-old Edmund responded, "Mommy, you are a sweet flower." Ed has always said that this much-needed compliment was capital in the bank which was drawn upon to make up for later transgressions.

Recently, in the light of Hillary Clinton's book which reasserts the old African proverb that it takes a whole village to raise a child, I have come to think of those early years and realize how little the "village" impinged upon our family life. Aside from our battles with the family to the north who were "Bahbawians" according to Edmund, and our happy relationship with the older couple next door and other mature families on the block, we lived in our own world, and our mothers, whatever they thought, respected our strongly held convictions, including the one that said when one child has a birthday only he should get presents, contrary to the practice of grandmothers, and that television was to be used only occasionally. I was a stay at home mom except for Saturdays. Thanks to the assistance of Ed's mother, Dr. Spaeth, and Aunt Margaret who came one day a week so that I could take the older children to Cenacle, and thanks to our extraordinary caretaker and friend, Mrs. Thelen, we were able to operate during those years, taking care of individual needs.

Soon after Rob was born in 1966, John became ill with a seeming flu. John had not wet his pants since he was two and when he did so again at three, I suspected a kidney infection. It was Friday and Dr. Spaeth knew I taught at Loyola on Saturday, journeying down to Lewis Towers after parking the car at the end of the "L" line at 63rd and Loomis. When I told him of John's thirst and incontinence, he asked if I could leave a urine sample at his door next morning on my way to the "L." That Saturday, I had promised to take Edmund and Mary Kate to school with me and we met Bob Konen, an old friend, at St. Mary's afterwards. Bob invited us all to lunch at Carson's Men's Grill, and we took a 3 p.m. train home.

The news that awaited us there was staggering. Dr. Spaeth had detected sugar in the urine sample and had called our house where Mrs. Thelen was caring for the children. He asked if the little boy could be brought to his office. Since Ed was home to take care of six-week-old Rob, Mrs. Thelen went off, with John and sidekick Joseph who was not going to miss an outing. By the time we got home, tests had been made at Little Company of Mary Hospital, and it was confirmed that John had diabetes.

A new chapter in our family's history had begun. I needed more help than ever for a while, for I, manually very clumsy, had to learn how to give John the daily injections. Dr. Spaeth explained that if I started giving John a daily shot, any three year-old would consider it a "cruel and unusual punishment." On the other hand, if John were to be hospitalized to determine the amount of insulin needed and then later told that he could return home if he would allow me to give him the daily injection, he would readily accept it. So, while

34 ~ The 1960s: A Family A' Building

various people like Aunt Margaret and Mrs. Thelen came each morning to send Mary Kate and Edmund off to school and take care of Joseph, aged two, and Baby Rob, I went off every morning to Little Company of Mary Hospital to practice. Whatever I learned, I demonstrated to Helen Thelen, and she became more adept than I at giving shots. I would go back later in the day to see John and one day Mom Kearney told me to stop at Carson Pirie Scott in the Evergreen Plaza and buy John the biggest teddy bear I could find. I did so, and Big Teddy became a permanent member of the family. When John came home a few weeks later, his exuberant spirit was as strong as ever. A call to Beverly Community Nursery School reassured us that they had no qualms about taking him back to the two-morning-a-week program, and life continued on. John never missed any event because of his diabetes and his obvious vigor discouraged anyone from ever suggesting that he limit his life. He was a fighter then as now.

XXXV
Robert

After my mother's death in 1965, it was hard to imagine that the apartment at 8146 Green was bereft of her presence. I would go there on Saturdays after my class at Loyola, ostensibly organizing her belongings for what Pat and I knew would ultimately be a sale of the property. The Kieltys, tenants and friends, still resided downstairs in Aunt Bessie's apartment and when Mrs. Kielty would hear me there on Saturday, she would put a fresh roll or piece of coffee cake outside the front door, ringing the phone to let me know it was there. She knew that mine was a sorrowful task and she wanted me to have a nourishing accompaniment to my instant coffee. Of such little acts of kindness as these we learn that though we have been temporarily separated from special people, the good that they did lives on. Certain things in my mother's house were where they had been since she had come as a bride of one year with my father and Baby Patrick. Some were to be taken to our home and others were to be sent to members of the family, as far away as Betty's place in Arcadia, Missouri. But at that time they were all in the places my mother had left them, and I reveled as well as wept in their presence.

Many years later, after the house had been long sold, I went back with my brother and my niece to make a visit. Most startling was that the built-in ironing board which my father had put in for my mother was now covered with cabinets. It was at the kitchen table next to this board where I had sat while Mom ironed her seemingly endless linen cloths and I read my school assignments to her during high school and college.

There we had discussed *Brideshead Revisited* after I read it aloud to her. She had told me that certain scenes like the seduction scene on shipboard would have been considered risqué in her era. Pressed for a comment on *Brideshead Revisited* in Father Weyand's class next day after my mother's remark, I sputtered out what my mother had said as an example of how sensibilities had changed. Father Martin D'Arcy

35 ~ Robert

was visiting our class that night in 1951 as a guest of Father Weyand. Father D'Arcy had been Rector of Campion Hall, Oxford, and had baptized Evelyn Waugh. The other students in "Catholic Renascence" felt rather sorry for me when I blurted out my rather parochial comment, but Father D'Arcy fixed his deep-set eyes on me and said, "Your mother would have made an excellent critic. That is the only scene I asked Waugh to leave out. But he did not agree and I didn't press the point." I knew I had my "A" and I blessed Father D'Arcy as I have every time since when I have passed the Martin D'Arcy Art Gallery at Loyola.

Well now that kitchen was changed, but I could still see the rather tall gray-haired woman standing there over snowy white linen which would cover the dining room table next time we had any kind of a familial gathering.

Soon we knew that Genevieve up in heaven had come through and was sending us another child who would, of course, be named for her beloved Robert if he turned out to be a boy, as our trend indicated. The day before Rob's birth, Joseph, twenty months, had been feeling poorly. So I phoned Dr. Spaeth, our wonderful pediatrician and friend whom I still talk to once in a while. When I told him that Joseph had a fever and that I thought I might be close to the time of delivery, he came right over. After examining the baby and giving him some antibiotics which he had brought along, he cheerfully made his way out telling us to be careful on that expressway down to Northwestern Memorial.

A colleague of Ed's—Bob Kovarik—was spending the night with us while his apartment was being redecorated so we knew that we could leave the sleeping children for an hour if Joseph was O.K. As the evening wore on, I knew that it was time to go, so we called our dear Mrs. Thelen who said her husband would drive her out to take care of the children. Robert Augustine Kearney was born early the next morning, so when the children woke up, Helen Thelen was able to tell them the news of their new brother. Mary Kate, six and a half, was not happy at the sex of her new sibling and would cheerfully have traded him in for any baby of the opposite sex. She soon changed her mind when Robert turned out to be the sweetest "smilingest" baby ever, ready to eat regularly.

Despite frequent colds and occasionally a high temperature, Rob seldom let ear infections spoil his appetite or his disposition, so he soon became known in the family as "Never Miss a Meal Kearney." But as time progressed, despite his obvious brightness, he was not talking. When I told him to put Daddy's socks away, to bring the newspaper, or to set Kate's book up in her room, he did so with seeming alacrity. But no speech. We made an appointment at the Northwestern audiology clinic and off Rob and I went to Chicago Avenue.

It was a familiar route, for that was where all of the children had been born. They had an ingenious device to use with non-talking toddlers. They put earphones on Rob and taught him how to pull the lever on what looked like a gigantic cash register when he heard a beep. He would be rewarded with a fruit loop which most children loved. There were further more precise tests and finally the audiologists told me he had a 33 percent hearing loss in both ears. They sent us to an ear, nose, and throat specialist, Dr. Hart, who prescribed medication for the build-up in his inner ear, probably caused by ear infections. Dr. Hart warned that this was a first step, but that surgery might still be necessary. He explained that while Robert was hearing what was going on, he did not hear sounds in the same way we did and consequently could not repeat them.

Robert did have the surgery in May when he was just over two and a half. In a then-unique arrangement, I was allowed to sleep next to his bed at Passavant Hospital so that he would not be frightened. Next day when they brought him back after the surgery to have his tonsils and adenoids removed and the fluid from his inner ear taken care of, a lunch tray was delivered for him by mistake. Ed had just arrived when the aide brought it in and remarked that we might as well eat the food since Rob would be allowed only soft food for awhile. When he saw his father start on the piece of chicken, Rob, hardly out of anesthesia, rose up from his bed and tried to grab the leg out of his father's hands. This perpetuated the reputation of "Never Miss a Meal Kearney."

Once home, the windows were opened and several birds perched on the bush outside the family room, singing their salute to the May sunshine. I saw Rob tense and then laugh at what he heard, and I knew that the surgery had been successful.

In the next months and years everybody taught Rob to talk. His fortunate position as youngest of five meant that he had the services of four older siblings, and each one made it his special mission to tutor "Robby." It was not hard, for he was a winsome child to whom people gave lollipops, balloons, and all manner of things, and he and I became a familiar sight in the local Jewel and local restaurants. There was a whole world Rob had to get to know and we were there to show it to him. When we went down for check-ups at Dr. Hart's we discovered a wonderful cafeteria in the new dental building on Chicago Avenue, and that is where "Never Miss A Meal Kearney" headed whenever we had an appointment. He went to nursery school at Beverly Community in the Unitarian Church and then to Sutherland where John was a third grader. The tuitions at Morgan Park Academy had become a burden, and we thought John's having a little brother at Sutherland would make it more attractive to him. Rob went to speech class there to make up for the language lag caused by his early hearing loss. When we asked him if other children left his class to attend this special help session, he answered, "Three people and a girl!"

As Rob grew up, he had his own unique style. Between seventh and eighth grade, we thought caddying might give an outlet for his excess energies but found, to our chagrin, that hanging around at the caddy shack at a local country club with other kids, hoping for a golfer, and hearing stories of other boys' real or imagined escapades were not the best thing for our big boy, entering his teens. Ed and I worried a lot, but a friend reminded us with humor and wisdom that we had a family way of operating and that reminding Rob that "Kearneys have a family tradition which dictates the way they act" was the way to go.

When Rob became thirteen that autumn and started eighth grade, he was immediately elected president of the middle school student council, and I saw a maturing in this "baby" of ours. I knew he had a firm hold on reality when he told me, in November, that he intended to take the test for St. Ignatius. Joseph was already making a mark for himself as No. 1 in the class two years ahead of Rob, and Edmund before him had graduated No. 3 in his class. Rob reassured me about any worry I might have had about him with the remark "I'm my own person; I won't try to be Joseph." Two years later when he was elected president of the junior class and the next year president of the Executive Board of the Student Council of St. Ignatius College Prep, I knew he was on solid ground.

That was the year that Joseph went off to Yale. John was at Northwestern, Edmund at Notre Dame, and Mary Kate in law school. Rob became our dependable chauffeur when I broke my arm that fall, even doing the grocery shopping. His wit reminded us more and more of my father and we knew that Robert had truly been the right name for our fifth and final child. A lawyer and caring individual today, he is still on hand when we need him and never without an R.S.-type riposte.

XXXVI
THE MIDDLE YEARS—
FAMILY AND PROFESSION

I continued to teach at Loyola on Saturdays through the '60s because, as Ed said, it gave me "surcease" from the demands of five children (all of whom in 1966 were under six-and-a-half years of age). I returned to full-time teaching in 1970 when my youngest was four and I had the chance to do the kind of work I do best—interacting with people in a setting where one gets to know students more in their persons than in their semicolon usage.

I have sometimes been asked if I felt any guilt at becoming what is now called a "working mom." My answer is that guilt is something felt when it is thought one should have done otherwise but didn't. I did what I believed important and necessary in the '60s. As the '70s came, I simply continued to do what I believed was right for all, for my family and myself. Society then and today is too judgmental.

An opportunity to do such teaching came in 1970. A long-time friend referred me to an opening at Pestalozzi-Froebel Teachers College, a ninety-year-old institution located in my (and my mother's) beloved Chicago Loop. The job was sardonically described as one in which "they're looking for someone who will give a lot of dedication for not very much money." I responded that "lots of downtown regardless of monetary reward is what I am best at" and that "my years of motherhood have given me lots of 'nurturing' practice I could use there." I knew in the '60s that spending time with dishes and diapers was my vocation. But when I once again saw, in Charles Williams's phrase in *All Hallow's Eve*, "The lights of the City," I just went bananas. Truly, as Ecclesiastes says, there is a season for everything.

"Downtown" was my inherited milieu. My mother loved her weekly foray to Marshall Field's. I was truly her daughter. Downtown—ah bliss! Concerts in the summer, and, sometimes even in the winter in the subway. And people of all kinds. There is the newspaperman outside the Randolph and Wabash "L" station who would run out of his booth to thrust the *Daily News* in my bag; the familiar faces at the noon Mass at St. Peter's and the discarded (sometimes by societal indifference, sometimes by personal circumstances) homeless, all part of this teeming "Vale of Tears" of which we are all a part. I dash past the windows of Carson's and Field's, past the flower sellers, momentarily see the lightpost banners of the season, scurry around the nightly line-up at the Berghoff on Adams, cut across the Federal Plaza, brave the seedy "flop houses" on Van Buren (now more sensitively to be called SROs—single-room occupancies) and, with a little bit of luck, I catch the 5:28 Rock Island train. If not, there is always the 5:55. But this nightly experience reduces itself to one thing—People. People always in motion. People always dashing. People. How wonderful.

One year after I joined the faculty of Pestalozzi-Froebel, it was absorbed by the historic National College of Education located in Evanston which wanted (as was then fashionable in those chaotic times) to establish an urban campus presence. I was asked to remain and received tenure in 1976. That is a story in itself. Perhaps someday my husband and advisor in the affairs of Academe will elaborate. It is a story reflective of the times. Suffice it to say here that, with the support of the President, Dr. Calvin Gross, I survived.

Thus, the "Urban Campus" with hundreds of students in several different programs made it, and in the sense of blending God's gift of a loving family with a profession that I love, I made it too. Though the money was not comparable to public education, I was able to help my five children through all those years of education until the youngest (Robert) is a "Notre Dame Lawyer," the oldest (Mary Kate) teaches law, with a clinical psychologist, Ph.D., and University Professor (Edmund), a Texas lawyer (John), and a soon-to-be Marquette University law professor (Joseph) in between. I was lucky, my field and my children's lives were really one: teaching and learning. My husband was an academic, a history professor at Chicago State University, so we as a family were blessed by a natural understanding of what each was doing and a respect for the obligations our commitments imposed on us.

Ed was supportive of my career. He understood the personal necessity I found in the "people" contact I found in teaching. Supportive in the broad sense but, also, in the lesser tasks, including putting the roast in the oven, preparing the salads, sending the kids for milk after school, and generally keeping tabs on all until I reached home after my long trip from downtown and sometimes from meetings in Evanston. As he once said while unpacking the dishwasher, "All in all, I'm less trouble than a domestic, more company than a dog, and cheaper than a gigolo."

Our lifestyles and values meshed well. In the precollege years, we all sat down—usually by 6:30—to eat dinner and then each went off to the evening's homework. Loads of wash were to be done, cookies were baked, and the following day's lunches were prepared. Nothing was really a big deal. We had a routine and I see now we used the KISS principle (keep it simple, stupid). We didn't have TV on during the week. It wasn't even a possibility because it would have provided too much of a temptation and distraction. We shared our lives and fought over Chicago politics at dinner and then went to our work. If by some rare chance you didn't have homework you were forced to find a book (I can see Joseph secreted on the basement steps) or in the case of John repair to your workshop downstairs. Horror of horrors, I can even see shadowy figures stealing in to watch a bit of TV in our bedroom. Thank God we were not perfect.

As the years went on, our work inevitably included rehearsals and plays for the thespian daughter, math and Latin contests for the sons, parent-teacher conferences (we always went as a duo and I don't think we ever missed—even one), and in later years, graduations. They were a command performance—voluntary for no one.

Interspersed were vacations, some more successful than others, but all forging the ties that bind in memories for a lifetime. Crystal Lake, Door County, Stevensville, Tulsa and the Kellys, Washington, D.C., Colonial Williamsburg, the Stratford Festival, and St. Louis and Missouri relatives. The years blur but the memories shine.* Raising our family was, as I tell my partner, "a good work," or less grammati-

---

* Editor's Note: Vacations maybe, but remember, Mary Jane did all the driving. For her, vacations were supreme acts of self-sacrifice.

cally but more emphatically, "we done good." Even the then (1986) eighty-four-year-old (and not uncritical) paternal grandmother who got her wheelchair placed early that Memorial Day to see her beloved grandson receive his classics degree, *summa cum laude*, at Yale, even she decided that I had been "successful."

We are proud of each other and nobody says, "I did it." We have tried to live by the principle that each has a responsibility to help the other because as we laughingly say, "That's what families do."

The kids will be paying off their loans for years. We put in what we could and will continue to help as much and in as many ways as we can. After all we did stack the cards in favor of education. It's our true legacy to them and one I hope they pass on.

As all do, we have lived through life's uncertainties. I think often of these uncertainties—how we all live borrowing trouble from the future. What a future-oriented life we live. Like Marcher, in James's *Beast in the Jungle*, we don't recognize how much love surrounds us. So, as in *Ferdinand*, I often tell my husband Ed, "Sit down and smell the flowers." By God's grace, we have had our share of roses to smell. I say that's not hedonistic, it's just good therapy.

Editor's Postscript—
Living, Loving, and Parting, 1990-1997

Mary Jane did not have an opportunity to write fully of her world of the '90s. I feel that I must, for her life though increasingly physically limited came, I believe, to a fullness of satisfaction in those seven years. The ordinariness of these years belies the fact of how supremely treasured they were.

I retired in January 1992 and Mary Jane was now teaching three days a week. After an operation to install a shunt in September 1992, she was off until January 1993. It turned out to be a mini-sabbatical, and much of her "Recollections" was written at that time. We were now together more than since our early marriage. Oakley House was perfect, she said, for "together separateness." She could write upstairs in the study, while I could occupy myself downstairs and periodically reinforce her with coffee. Lunches together (Oak Lawn Restaurant a strong No. 1); forays out shopping; for her, coffee and reading on the deck; sojourns in the Beverly (her favorite) and Oak Lawn libraries; family dinners on many Sundays as in-gatherings of a now-scattered clan took place—all of these in the words of a song of our era gave a strange excitement to a very mature "Nearness of You." Mary Jane continued her interest of many years in recent immigration, giving frequent welcoming addresses to newly naturalized citizens at their induction ceremonies, always encouraging them to continue their pursuit of higher education. Her love of people was evidenced in her fascination at the constantly expanding cultural mosaic of America.*

And in these years a few moments of travel: a theater weekend with Mary Kate in New York in 1994; two trips to Montana and one to Washington, D.C.; the last included a personally guided tour of the Supreme Court and a witnessing of a case being heard by the Court, courtesy of our son, Joseph, who at the time (1996) was clerking for

---

* Cf. Part Two, Chapter XII.

Justice Antonin Scalia. Montana (1993 and 1995) was a rediscovery of a summer of my childhood. I had gone to Montana in the summer of 1934 to recuperate from the paralysis that had laid me waste the previous year. With my Aunt Margaret, I spent two months on the ranch of two Irish bachelor uncles who had homesteaded in the first decade of the century. They returned to Ireland in 1936, selling the ranch to their "neighbors" (several miles away) the Dear family. In 1993, Joseph determined to renew "his" Montana roots, researched the Dear family, and incredibly reestablished a relationship with truly wonderful people.

At his urging, we "did" Montana, including the "Dinneen Ranch," "Glacier," "the Drive to the Sun," and more. Mary Jane fell in love with the West, and we revisited Montana in 1995. You can truly go home again—1934, 1993, and 1995. But no matter how short or long our trips, Mary Jane's invariable comment on our return was, "It was fine, but it was one day too long."

And marriages. Edmund's to Cris in the fall of 1988; John's to Linda in November 1992; and Joseph's to Anne in August 1996—all gave her satisfaction and delight as did her certainty that Mary Kate and Deryck were soon to embark on their pilgrimage. While that left Robert unaccounted for, she often told me that I needn't fear for R.S. Grogan's heir, in name and charm.

Beyond all, our grandchildren, thus fulfilling the marital wish of "your children's children."

Not all of them, perhaps, for her work goes on. The words of Belloc are truer today than when I first read them to her in 1957:

> For you shall make récord, and when that's sealed
> In Beauty made immortal, all is healed.

With God's help, her first date's challenge to me of wanting a dozen children might yet be reached, and exceeded, in future generations.

The '90s included golden moments. They fulfilled and completed Mary Jane's realization of a life that reflected the words of her favorite biblical quotation from the Book of Proverbs, "Who shall find a valiant woman—She is worth more than jewels," and they fulfilled our mutual promise to build a life whose legacy would be in Belloc's words: "Children for memory : the Faith for pride : / Good land to leave : And young Love satisfied."

My Life: A Conversational Memoir

Mary Jane Grogan (1934)

Marion Gleason, Mary Jane Grogan, Alice Gerrity

With R.S. (ca. 1943)

In New Orleans (ca. 1950)

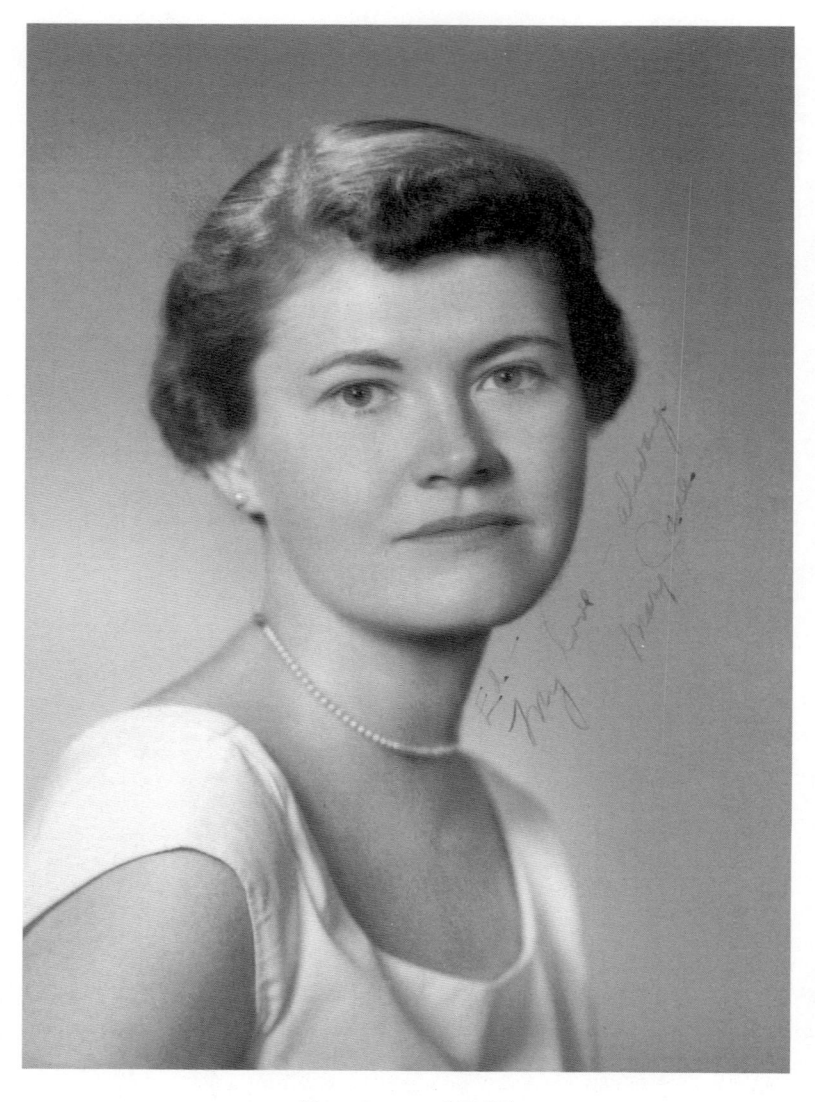

Engagement (1957)

My Life: A Conversational Memoir 145

July 26, 1958

Mary Jane Kearney

My Life: A Conversational Memoir 147

Mary Jane & Dad

Mary Jane & Mom at End of Wedding Reception

Holding John, Expecting Joseph (1964)

In Front of 10127 S. Oakley Ave. with Mary Kate & Edmund

1967 Christmas Card: Robert, Mary Kate, Edmund, Joseph, John

Ed & Mary Jane (ca. 1973)

*At Loyola University Class of '52 Reunion (1977)
Mary Ellen & Jack Clark, John Gerrietts (Chairman of the Loyola English Department), Mary Jane & Ed*

Family at Joseph's Graduation in New Haven (1986)

154 Mary Jane Kearney

Ed & Mary Jane (1986)

My Life: A Conversational Memoir

With Students Just off Michigan Ave. Between Monroe & Madison

Mary Jane with Her Brother, Patrick Grogan (1987)

Marion (Gleason) Sullivan, Mary Jane Kearney, Phyllis Trueblood, Alice (Gerrity) Kelly (1988)

My Life: A Conversational Memoir

With Robert at His Graduation in South Bend (1988)

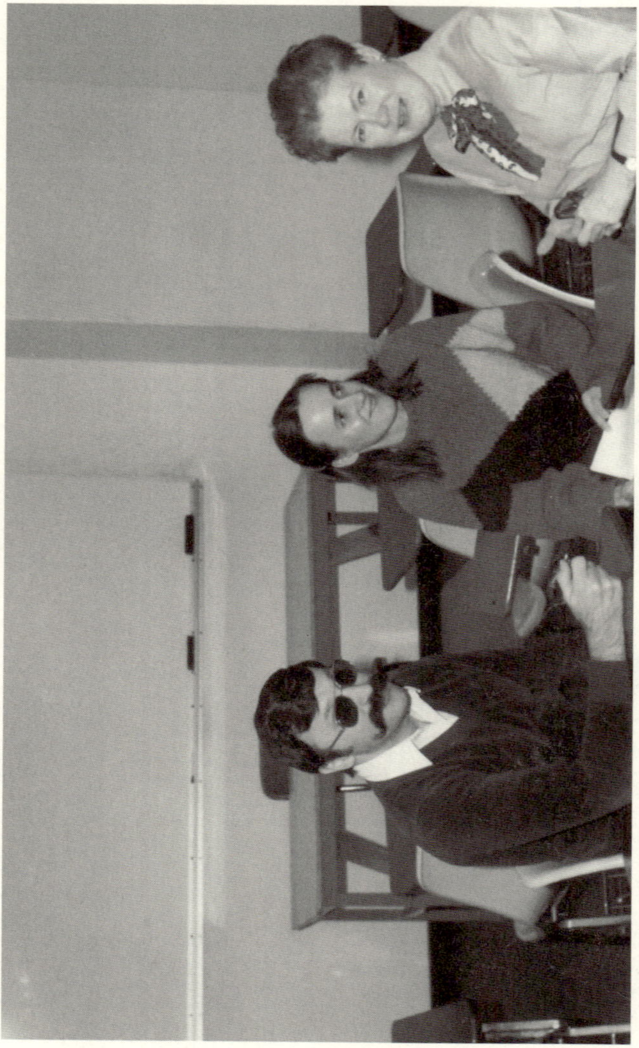

Teaching at National College of Education

My Life: A Conversational Memoir 159

Birthday Party (1990)

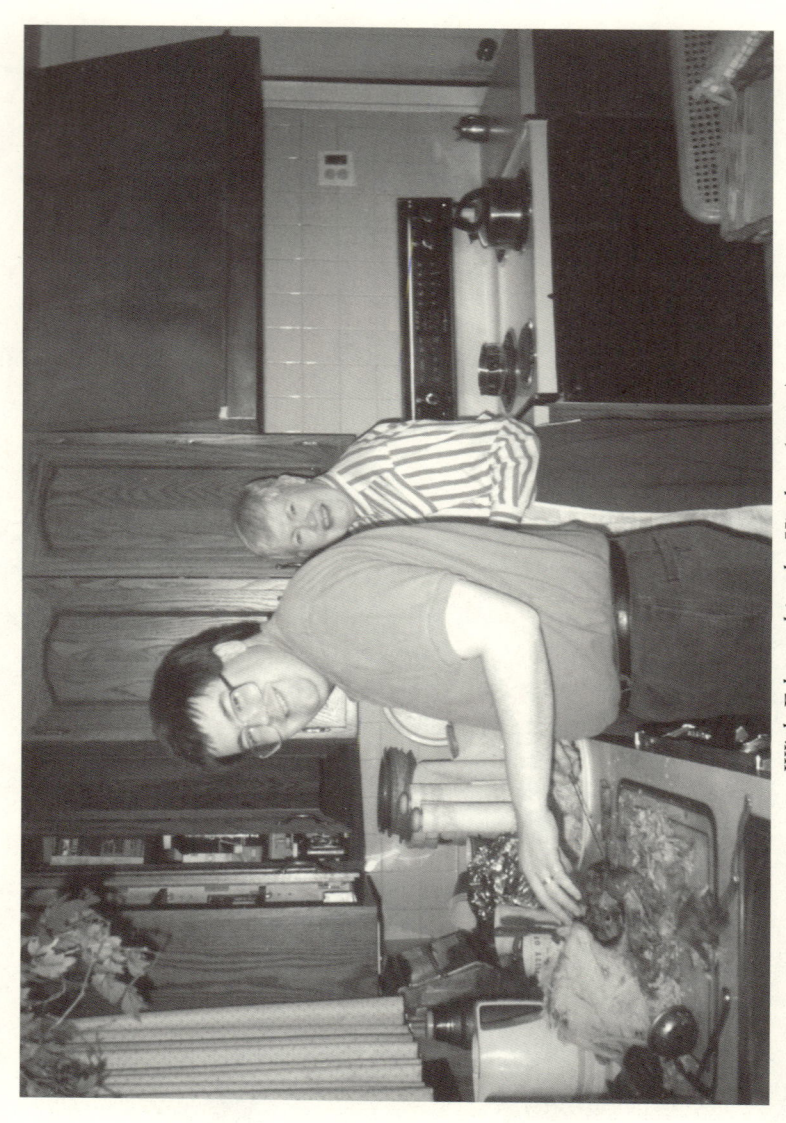

With Edmund in the Kitchen (1993)

Mary Jane & Ed (1993)

With Mary Kate (1993)

With John (1993)

With Joseph & Ed on the Dinneen/Dear Ranch in Montana (1993)

In Montana (1995)

PART TWO

Editor's Note—
Musings, Vignettes, and Essays

These writings, in unintended ways, supplement Mary Jane's memoirs, throwing light on the workings and traditions of our family. In that sense, some might be called "personal" essays. Note, among others, "Misty: a Fond Remembrance," "Rescuing Family Heritage," "The Back to School Party," "Thoughts on Delivering a Son—To College," and "Some Things in Life—And at Notre Dame—Keep Repeating."

Some of Mary Jane's writings were what she termed "musings," others were "vignettes," and some represented the classic essay. The first two here fit neatly into none of these categories. They justify themselves and are part of "promises kept." I include the first essay, written by Mary Jane in high school on "The Most Unforgettable Character I've Met," not simply because she wrote it or because she kept it or because it is especially sparkling. I include it because it is true. Robert Stephen Grogan was, also in my life as his son-in-law, the most unforgettable character I've met.

When he died in 1960, I promised Mary Jane we would keep his memory alive. I know that was a promise kept. He and I had a special relationship—all too sadly brief. He gave me wise, but unobtrusive, counsel and, most of all, he gave me his most special love, his daughter. I can still see him on our wedding day as I looked back getting into the car after Mass. He was standing on the top of the church steps and as we waved, he clutched his breast as if to remove his heart and threw it to me. It is a memory of both joy and pain. In all possible ways, he must be remembered.

I
The Most Unforgettable Character I've Met (ca. 1948)

Some of my earliest recollections are, quite naturally enough, of my father. But these recollections are not ordinary ones, for my father is far from an ordinary man. He belongs to that distinguished class most popularly known as characters.

Even in his very early life, it has often been said that he evidenced certain undeniable characteristics of a born executive. On Saturdays, it was his express duty to scrub half, no more, of the kitchen floor and for this task he received one cent (which in those days bought no end of delicious goodies and was almost too much to be spent in a single store). However, my illustrious father would offer his penny to his younger brother, Jim, to do his work along with his own. This offer was usually spontaneously accepted for my Uncle Jim was not too proud to accept and certainly was too sweet-hungry to refuse. Meanwhile, my father would efficiently take up the task of being chief executive of the clean up squad.

But, however, as often happens, my father grew up.

Finally, the day dawned when my father was to try for his first job. Great was his faith in the benevolent patron of Ireland, St. Patrick, and it was with a fervent prayer in his heart and a jaunty green tie on his neck that he set out on that early St. Patrick's morn. Needless to say, St. Patrick smiled down upon my father right through the eyes of his prospective employer, for his mission was accomplished.

One of the happiest of Father's many happy faculties has always been his ability to descend to the level of the tiniest child, both physically and mentally. When in demand, as he usually was at a party, he could often be found sitting on the floor with the juveniles, spinning yarns of interminable proportions and thoroughly enjoying them himself. Great were these products of his ever fertile imagination and many a grown person today cherishes memories of his immortal Beevo Bosco Booze Kettle.* My first lessons in life and human nature, I learned from my father, and never forgotten are these words with which he advised me when I went to him with my childish problems: "Your friends need no explanations; your enemies will not believe them anyway."

Memorable are the Christmases which were always made especially festive through the efforts of Dad. He worked tirelessly with decorations and it was through his lifelike Bethlehem cribs that my brother and I realized the beauty of that first Christmas.

Often at parties or small gatherings, Dad will smash all formality with his silly little ditties. Once while having dinner with some of Mother's "shirt tail" relations, he broke out with, "of all my wife's relations, I like myself the best."

Dad carries his lightness of touch over into his everyday relations. Though he may be weighted down by business worries, never a trace of irritability or pettiness is carried into his home. Surely he fulfils this motto penned by Edgar A. Guest: "Beyond this door shall never go / The burdens that are mine to know. . . . Only the good shall go with me / For their devoted eyes to see."

The position which Dad has always held in the estimation of our friends is remarkable. He is as the youngest of the young in heart and always ready to join any comical prank. Father's impulsiveness has always been a standard joke among us. One night when we had company, he graciously bid adieu to the guests and then immediately proceeded to switch off all the lights. By the time our visitors reached the street, the house was in complete darkness and gave the impression of being wholly uninhabited.

Whenever I see a swing, I will think of my father, I will remember the happy Sunday mornings we spent, he, my brother, and I, just swinging and enjoying the beauty of the things around us.

---

* Editor's Note: These were tales told off "the top of his head" of an imaginary little boy who got himself into dangerous or embarrassing predicaments. I take some pleasure in adding to the lore the alliterative fact that Beevo was blessed with a "big blue bondoonie." The last was Dad's term for anyone's backside.

1 ~ *The Most Unforgettable Character I've Met (ca. 1948)*   171

And, whenever I see a train, I will recall the excitement with which he invited us to watch it roll by, always "counting the cars."

When I see a sled whisking down the slippery incline of a hill, I'll remember my first introduction to the great sport of "wintering" through Dad.

When I see report cards, I'll remember how he always jestingly said, "I always got at least one hundred and ten percent."

But, most of all, I'll remember him when I see happy people. I'll remember him because he has been one of the happiest of persons, full of his own happiness and extending it in many large and small ways to others.

My father has had little to do with my formal education and yet from him I learned some of my most valuable lessons. I would not exchange for anything what he has attempted to give me through his example, through his blessed secret of living by the day.

II
Remembrances of a Practical Giver
(ca. 1991)

It is raining, almost sleeting today, and I am working in an upstairs room, called a "study" partially to invest it with the mystique which the connotations of that word impart. A moment ago, I needed to attach two sheets of notes together so I reached for the black and silver stapler which resides almost forgotten in a drawer here.

All of a sudden, I was in another room and it was forty years ago, a porch which was my college bedroom, abandoned by my recently married brother and never as well heated as the rest of the house. That did not bother me at twenty and, as my dad was wont to say, "Its temperature helps keep the head clear during late study hours."

However, the moment I am remembering was not late at night but early in the morning of my twenty-first birthday.

At six-thirty, it was only a few minutes before my father would descend, lunch box in hand, to the garage he rented from the man across the alley, to take his car out and drive to work. As president of a concrete products company, he didn't need to carry his lunch, but he did so because he didn't want to take time out to go to a restaurant for lunch and because he always had done so. He came out to my porch, that twenty-first birthday morning, handed me the brown-wrapped package, and said, "I think you're old enough to have one of these of your own." It was a hand-held stapler and I used it today with a rush of memories of the dear practical man who had given it to me.

His gifts were almost always of a practical nature. When my mother had a broken arm, he found a grabber so that she could get things from a top shelf without mounting a ladder. He presented it to her as though he were giving her diamonds.

2～Remembrances of a Practical Giver (ca. 1991)

On his way home from work, my father often stopped at a convent which had a chapel accessible to the public to say a prayer. Seeing a small sister repeatedly lug a large wooden ladder around to replace light bulbs and decorate the chapel for religious feasts, he called her aside one day to say, "Sister, I'm going to buy you one of those lightweight aluminum ladders they have now to make your work easier." Perhaps it was the idea of making her life easier that caused this penitential lady to object, but she did, giving him a list of other gifts, however, that would be welcome.

My father's habit of giving unorthodox gifts continued during the early days of my marriage. Having helped us find the house we were living in, my father stopped in at least once a week, ostensibly "to use the plumbing." In reality, he came to bring some of the things new homeowners need, like a bucket, a chamois, or a step-stool, and they were always welcome.

He brought his Chinese laundryman who did his shirts several rubber stamps with which to identify patrons' packages, and I never knew whether it was out of deference or great Oriental courtesy that my father had his own stamp behind the counter bearing the symbols "P3."

Little wonder it is that I tend to give very mundane, often unglamorous, gifts for showers and birthdays and need to be helped by salespeople and children when I purchase wedding presents. My actions are part of the tradition of the man who visited my room early that morning of my twenty-first birthday with his brown-wrapped gift and the words, "I think you're old enough to have one of your own."

III
A Mother Left Holding the Bag

Recently, I stopped in at a well-known Chicago department store, renowned for its quality merchandise and enlightened employment practices and—in our family—for its plastic shopping bags. They were two-ply, rather roomy carry-alls capable of being closed at the top with a drawstring. You know the kind—they bore pictures in black or brown of Chicago landmarks built by the city's pioneers. They were at once useful and a tie to a shared past.

I blithely made my way to the second floor, plunked down my dollar bill, and said in a resonant voice, "Four plastic shopping bags please!" To my dismay, disgust, and despair, I heard, "Oh we've given up making those. We have some nice paper shopping bags." With that, she offered me a bag whose path to obsolescence was about one hour. Though I in no way resembled Oliver when he approached the beadle for more porridge, I certainly felt like him as I mouthed, "But *pleeze*, our family needs these."

How could she know, this clerk of twenty-one, that one of these bags had carried a pair of comfortable shoes to the church lo those many years ago so that I could wear them during the hours-long reception later? Could she ever have taken two of them with her in the days before pampers, one for wet and one for dry, on a long summer outing? Surely, she had never grabbed one from the cabinet for gym togs which had to be clean and fresh or bring a dreaded loss of points for a class team. And, as each child went off to college and came home for weekends, she must not have known that this was the extended, expandable suitcase and carrier of freshly made cookies. How could she know? She was just too young, I guess.

But I wonder what her memories will be. For we all will have memories. They are the ribbons of our lives, tying us to our past. Some of them are plastic-bag-like, trivial. Some are of great import. All are part of our whole.

IV
On Boys, Boudoirs, and Boobies

There is something about a plastic bag which makes a small child want to put it over his head—I know not what! As the mother of five such darlings in the '60s, I was well-warned by manufacturers and friends of the hazard, so I immediately tucked the bag which I had found on my front doorstep, holding a sample or encasing a new set of kitchen utensils, into the highest and safest place in my kitchen. One day I had a pocketless dress and was near no such place so I tucked it down in my bra for safe keeping.

That night when I was getting ready for bed, I laughingly discovered my stowaway and told my husband about it. He made some remark like "your boobies need no plastic," in the privacy of our bedroom. But little pitchers have big ears and one son, always later known for his nocturnal study habits, must have overhead us chuckling.

Soon afterward, I was at a public playground with all five of the children and I had a new set of sand toys with me. As I took them out of the voluminous plastic bag warning signals went up in my brain. I did not want to set the bag down for even a minute. Since I had a sleeping infant on my arm, I surreptitiously tucked it into my bosom. I heard loud, and clear across the playground, "Mommy always puts her plastic bags in there even though Daddy says she doesn't need them." Moral: One is always teaching by example—but in the bedroom?

V

On the Enjoyment of the Mundane: An October Morning

An alarm clock sounds vaguely in some prehistoric land; not mine, I turn over. Eons later—or is it minutes—I realize no responsive morning sound has emitted from the room above. I rise; I mount the steps and speak. The responder shrieks—in what language I know not—that she has overslept and pleads for a ride to the train since the one intended has long gone. I am munificent—I have the day off!

As I wipe the early morning mist from the wagon, parked outdoors, always, because of its 1986 dimensions and a 1928 garage, a bird hails me. Did he say "cuckoo" or "bob white" or "caw"? I'm not sure, but he saluted my early morning industry with some of his own. Smart guys, those early birds.

The sun is fast coming up—I never noticed how washed it is that early. Daughter flies out of the house. "I'll drive," she says. More time for me to use this new found sensory perception. Papers are plopping onto porches—a hooded figure, sexless, throws them there; its eyes are hooded too, afraid I might intrude into its early morning absorption. I count the squirrels in the once-wooded neighborhood. There are thirty-four. Dutch Elm disease did not conquer all.

One maple at the corner is on fire; another has dismissed its foliage. No crackle underneath the trees this year because of so much water, just swoosh. Two red-and-yellow-clad joggers pass. They belong to this new army whose mandatory attire is hooded knit and drawstrings.

The train comes—we make it and I turn the car around. Neighbors leaving for work look questioningly toward me, an alien at this hour. I wonder if they will be encased until dark and I want to call, "Don't go!" I refrain—my family has to live here. I re-enter the house and put on my coffee. The paper invites; the apples gleam in the bowl; last night's dishes wait to be unpacked. I don't care.

I want all mornings to be this way but I know that tomorrow the birds may not call to me, the squirrels may not smile, and the fiery autumn tree may be bare. Or perhaps I will not notice them.

VI
Reflections on Mutual Pilgrimages

The bum was on that cold Chicago corner every day that winter of my broken arm. I got a ride with a friend to the "L" and came out of the tube just where he was standing, near St. Peter's Church in the Loop. He got whatever was left in my pocket which I dropped into his cup with my one good hand. People talk to you when you have an injury, and he opened up about his plans to be independent, his arthritic pains, and the much worse state of people in the shelter where he slept nightly. I responded with the difficulties of teaching today's unprepared students, the problems of paying for five children's educations, and the one thumb sticking out of my cast which I couldn't get warm.

One morning he looked different. To my greeting he responded, "Today I have something for you." From the recesses of his coat he extracted a *Wall Street Journal,* saying with a twinkle, "Since I see that you're into investments, I think you need this!" As I dashed into St. Peter's he called, "Say hello to the Lord," and the full impact of his remark reached me. I was making an investment every day of my life and he had given me something to remind me of it.

I saw him again the other day—he was selling papers this time and said things were better for him. I told him I remembered his cheerfulness that winter when I was in plaster and he was restricted in another way. We parted, I to my teaching job, he to sell the rest of his papers. I will never know his name and it doesn't matter. We had shared, briefly, that kind of camaraderie which comes from knowing we're both on a pilgrimage and each of us walked a little more jauntily because of this knowledge. Maybe all the way to heaven can't be heaven, but it can certainly be a little easier when we help each other along.

VII
A World Programmed to Say "No!"

The voice on the other end of the line was impersonal but faintly pleasant. I was calling my daughter's charge card company to find out if her check had reached it. She had been a little late sending it in, and charge card interest rates are much too high to miss a payment. When an overdue notice arrived, I offered to investigate the matter. Surely, I thought, the computer just hadn't caught up with the account. The check, this time, was indeed in the mail.

"What may we help you with, ma'am?"

"I would like to know if a check arrived to square my daughter's account, please. She received an overdue notice, you see."

"I'm sorry, ma'am."

"Sorry?"

"We cannot release such information."

"Which information is that?" I asked, not entirely without sarcasm and with visions of my mail impounded and the word "classified" holding it hostage.

Ten minutes and two supervisors later, I found out that the check did indeed arrive. "I really don't think it's against any law I know of," I was still mumbling when the voice piped, still brightly, "The check has arrived." I mustered a feeble and insincere thank you and re-entered the real world.

And then there was the employee in the department store who told me that they had no more sweaters, period.

"Excuse me, but this sweater here, would you have any of—"

"No, ma'am."

"—these in a different color?"

"Oh, well, I don't think so, no."

"Yes, ma'am," said another man, "I think we do have them in another color." He was smiling, and I knew he must be the manager to be so well-informed.

After all of this, it just seemed inevitable that a battle of the "no's" would take place. And it did. I drove to the hospital with my husband to pick up his aunt, who was an outpatient. I drove into the hospital circle, my husband went in, and I moved up a bit. Soon there was a tap at the car window. She was dressed in a uniform.

"You cannot park here."

"But, I'm not parking," I explained.

"You cannot leave the car here."

"I'm just waiting for my husband's aunt. You see, he just went in to pick her up. They'll be right out, I'm quite sure."

"No. You must move the car."

"Where?"

"There is a parking garage."

"Oh no. I'm not going to pay for parking I don't need. She is going to be right out, and then I'll be sitting in a parking garage." No, I thought, that just doesn't seem logical at all.

"You will not move your car?"

Now was my big chance. Besides, through the rear-view mirror I could see them coming already. "No," I told her.

"Humph!" said she incensed, and then got on her walkie-talkie.

Oh, it goes on and on. The grocery boy with no more paper plates, the ticket man with no more lower level seats. ("Oh, yes, well it seems we do have some.")

"No," you see, is the easy answer and doesn't necessarily mean "No," however strange that may seem. It may mean, "Go away, I'm tired," or, "We have our rules, so that we can obviate any assumption of individual responsibility," or, "Our bureaucracy is too irrational to rethink this matter," or—the possibilities are open-ended, aren't they? It could even become absurd someday: "No" might come to really mean "Yes."

"Come here, Johnny. How would you like to go to the zoo today and see all of those amazing animals you love so much? . . . No? Good! You get your sister and I'll start the car."

VIII
Fifty Years Later

We were fifty years out of grade school (1944), and we were having a reunion. A reunion one would say of those parish-centered, ghetto-like lives some had accused us of living. We were ethnic Catholics of the '30s and '40s. And here we were, having survived in the real world in spite of our former cocoon-like existence.

Those who had predicted a cultural immersion disaster for us in the "real world" couldn't have been more wrong. We were that evening a group of Americans who had "made it" (or maybe "billed it") in a variety of ways, as did others of our Depression–war–post-war generation. We came together to engage in mutual nostalgia and well-wishing nearing our mid-sixties. Most of our battles had been fought but the final one—death was still ours. Sadly, we missed some who had already fought that battle. Given our faith, perhaps more than we should have; but, perhaps, because of our age, did we begin to hear "time's wingèd chariot"?

Impressions are scattered. One guy remembered me as one of the "smart girls." We laughed. It was irrelevant and had been for a long time. If not culturally diverse, we had become vocationally diverse. We had businessmen, teachers, quite a number, one priest (a vocation produced in spite of stern-faced preachers who appeared in the 1940s at vocation Sundays and lured fresh-faced boys to minor seminaries in Wisconsin or Iowa where their calling could be "nurtured"), a few lawyers, but no doctors that I know of. Did that emanate from the lack of science orientation as would be attributed by some, or were we only an atypical example? There certainly has not been a dearth of South Side doctors in our generation. Nevertheless, science was hardly a feature of our curriculum. I remember the pile of science books on a table in front of the classroom—undisturbed and inviolate during the week and passed out willy-nilly on Fridays—if we had time.

Whether we had gone on to college and in some cases beyond or gotten a job directly out of high school, we were well-prepared, though not exceedingly well-prepared, educationally—unless, of course, one considers our world-class mastery of the linking verbs or the variety of prepositions we had mastered. We were much better prepared in our little ethnic enclave to handle the English language than the world's propositions. Then, or was it later, we were instructed that those propositions were "out there," but in our world there were no gradations—not even the now apocryphally remembered "above the neck" and "below the neck." All propositions were mono-purpose. The gradations of human conduct we had in future years to learn for ourselves.

But it was a simple world. Fighting a global war and clear tyranny, "good" and "bad" were absolutes. It was a world of paper drives, tinfoil collections, meat rationing, and the always available fill-in: Spam. Our world was a world of authoritarianism, of rigid structure, of pastors and teachers who told us we had to attend the children's Mass on Sunday or be suitably punished for what would be judged an act of defiance (in truth, I don't remember how). Outside the church on Sundays, Father Coughlin's increasingly anti-Semitic paper, *Social Justice*, was hawked with its message of a global Jewish capitalist conspiracy, while inside the pastor preached against it. Before the paper was suppressed by the government, at the beginning of the war, it found some but not a great deal of support in an ethnically Irish neighborhood with its message that the war raging in Europe was in fact the last stand of British imperialism.

When we graduated (June 1944), my father (R.S.—Bob to my mother, Rob to many, for whom our youngest son Rob is named) laughingly offered me a "bonus" if I would tell the class banquet about the terrible and quite unsanitary school bathrooms. Of course, he knew I wouldn't and, well constrained as we had been trained to be, couldn't talk about a parish situation as "insignificant" as not being able to go to the bathroom all morning long on cold days after most of us had walked six blocks. To say anything negative would, we knew, have been "disloyal." Questioning of any authority or of authority's works was not part of our training.

We were the first generation in our families to have a completely Catholic education, and we smugly knew we were better than the "publicks." We had the besieged minority's conviction that we were better than those "others." So what if the bathrooms didn't work—or that we couldn't use them when by off-chance they were in working order. One simply accepted, publicly, of course, but privately as well. The situation was a family matter, and those in authority knew best.

IX
WE ALWAYS GO TO BED ANGRY

The program signed off with a final bit of wisdom from the long-married and much-revered author: "So don't go to bed angry; make sure you understand each other before you turn off the light." Such is the popular and often professional advice, but after twenty-seven years of marriage and with hopes of more good ones to come, I beg to disagree. That guy or gal whose sight you can't bear right now won't look nearly so threatening after a night's sleep and a good cup of coffee in the morning as he did when he said, "We're spending too much money," or "I don't want to go to the Donovans' on Saturday; I don't like them."

It is a simple principle of elementary psychology that a bit of withdrawal from an emotion-charged confrontation enables one to look at the matter afresh. It's the "take a breath and count to ten" principle expanded. For some reason, this is never applied to marital tiffs. Now we would all admit that there are a few disagreements which need to be argued out because of immediate consequences, but most of the time they don't need to be exhausted now—not when you are too.

After we were married a year, eons ago, my husband chortled one day, "You know—all of our arguments take place after 10:30 p.m. Do you think that's because you're a morning person, apt to be crabby at night, dear?" My answer was in kind, "No, that's because you have been practicing all day being so nasty to your European Civilization students, that you can't be civilized at home."

But that semi-playful exchange started me thinking and I began to keep score. Sure enough, of seven arguments in the next four weeks, six were late at night. Now we had been following the principle of "Let's clear the air" and found we lost a lot of sleep. As the children would begin to come along, we no longer would be able to continue the quest for understanding into the wee hours. Indeed, we found after children that, by the time we reached our "understanding" (or finished our argument), it was time for the little ones to wake up—Ugh!

So we devised a time limit for ourselves. If we couldn't settle it within five minutes, we'd postpone it. One Sunday we said we'd have to have our differences settled by the time Masterpiece Theater came on—because neither of us wanted to miss that. Once we watched *The Forsythe Saga* in two different rooms, but watch it we did. This meant, of course, that we were not arguing and were thinking of problems other than our own. There was a time, I admit, that we forgot by the next day what it was that we were fighting about. Usually that doesn't happen, but sometimes the issue that stood so large last night is considerably diminished after the toddler has poured oatmeal into the toaster or the man down the street has stopped in to say a neighbor has dropped dead. I guess the word is "perspective."

Now we are not usually incompatible, but we have had some good arguments. However, they have never been so bad that we can't go to sleep. After all, even the Lord rested following His labors creating the world, before He went on to managing it. I certainly think we humans could take a page from that book.

X
Misty: A Fond Remembrance

Today, I brought my eleven-year-old cat to the hospital. I don't think we will ever bring her home, although the veterinarian neighbors will do all they can to get her kidneys functioning again. Mingled with the sadness of her likely passing is a kaleidoscope of memories, "catapulting" as she did through our years.

She was known at first as the "raffle kitty" because she came home with me from a meeting of "mothers of children with diabetes." We were having a fund raiser for the summer camp and after the last roll of tickets was distributed, she was at the bottom of the box. Yes, the chairman confessed, she was the last one of the litter that she couldn't find a home for, and she brought her along "just in case one of you ladies . . . ."

I took her home and put her box in the warm steamy bathroom, the same kind of room her owner said she had been born in. But that was only the first of ten or eleven rooms of our old, rambling house which she conquered by exploration. One night we had to keep guests waiting as we removed a kitchen cabinet and got her out from behind it. "After all," said the eight-year old, "who could eat when Kitty was caught?" Another night we were awakened by a sleepy five-year old who told us that a ghost or "kitty" was stuck in his dresser drawer, which was jammed in tightly. It was Kitty, and we were saved from poltergeists and suffocated cats that night.

Cats, like mothers of small children, eat a little at a time whenever they can. Accordingly, our cat turned up for each breakfast from 6:00 a.m. on and saw all off to school. Meanwhile, she did her rounds exploring and then napped wherever her peregrinations led her. But she was right on hand at 3:30 when the school bus stopped and later, when the kids took the CTA, she seemed to know just when to wait for each homecoming. We always said she "counted the house" every night, for one time when our daughter, the oldest, was away for an extended time, it took Misty two weeks to accept each night that everybody was home who was coming home.

Someone once said that animals help us to be human, and Misty certainly did. With four boys, it is easy for manners to become rough, gestures hardly gentle. That couldn't happen with Kitty, because she was always coming around for a love or a rub, or you'd find her reclining on *her* desk chair just when you were going to sit down in it. I was told that she was especially inspiring with Latin translations. One boy said, "Did Caesar have a cat? I'll bet there was a cat who sat at the feet of Vergil and Horace during the reign of Augustus!" She sent them off to college, one by one, and recently when she became ill, one child had the temerity to venture that Kitty might have seen the college application for the youngest being prepared and thought her job was over. "Doesn't she know that I need her now more than ever?" I stormed. "How can I finish correcting those essays when she's not there to lie down on the ones I've done? Doesn't she know that I need a pair of green eyes and a bounding body to greet me now that you are all pursuing your destinies elsewhere most of the year? How can she think of abandoning me?"

Well, Kitty, we're sorry for all the times we had to lock you up when our allergic friends visited, and we hope you understood when we gave you your own bedroom upstairs on Saturday night so you wouldn't feel that you had to awaken us at the regular 5:45 on Sunday morning. We see now that kittens, like the children who love them, have a way of growing older. We hope you can stay with us awhile yet, but if you can't we want to say thank you—thank you for all the humanizing which your gentle, frolicsome, long-suffering feline ways did for us. You are part of the way we were, and because of you, we're a little nicer today.

XI
Rescuing Family Heritage

Although family stories such as how Grandpa got his first job on St. Patrick's Day and thereafter honored the memory by taking a rare annual holiday were often chuckled over, we realized that many wonderful heritage tales might be forgotten because the younger generation was not always ready to listen when we were in a mood to talk.

Almost everyone we know says "I wish I had asked more about where my family lived when they arrived from Europe," or "I wish I had asked Grandma about her brothers and sisters." But this year we decided to "take arms" as Shakespeare said, not against "a sea of troubles," but against insecurities of memory. We created our own quiz on family memories, ranging all the way from the oldest participant (Grandma) to the youngest I.Y.A. (Independent Young Adult, of course). The LOC (Loveable Old Curmudgeon, aka Father) conducted the first quiz based on his memories of family, friends, and relatives and stories of our children's early years—years which we had almost but not quite buried. The questions ranged from "To what local pizza place was a cab sent to bring home a high school girl who had gone there sans parental permission after a Friday basketball game at school?" to "What was the story which shocked the second-grade teacher in composition class so much that she returned it in an envelope marked 'Imaginative!'?" And there was the name of the educator who threatened to phone somebody's parents about missing third-grade assignments but failed to get through because the phone in the laundry room was mysteriously left off the hook after school for several days.

All of these and more turned up in our nightly 1985-86 holiday "whosits and whatsits" and turned that just-after-dinner period into hours of hootin' hilarity. We learned a lot about our family history, laughed a lot about our shared frailties, and hoped a lot for the coming year. Oh yes, we could submit our own questions to the LOC too, and sometimes he used one or two of them. As our last departing child called back to us from the front walk, "Don't lose my question, Dad. It's a good one." And we agreed. It had been a good one indeed—the idea, the holiday, and his question.

XII
ANOTHER VIEW
OF FOREIGN CAB DRIVERS

"Do you know what it is to have your skin on fire? To be burning up and not be able to run away from it? When I saw the flames leaping up at the Waco Compound yesterday on television, I knew that was happening to children and I cried. I have children."

The dark-haired man turned and faced me as we came to a stoplight and his eyes glistened with tears. He was one of the foreign cab drivers I have gotten to know over several months since a return to teaching after surgery meant I had to use cabs during the months of inclement weather—longer this year than usual. Now this driver went on to discuss further what we all saw in horror. He was cautiously critical of the procedure and we both listened attentively to a commentator on National Public Radio, the station he had tuned to in his cab.

This incident reminded me that in the period that I've been relying on cabs, I've seen another side of "those foreign cab drivers" than the image so often mocked in conversation for their lack of precise knowledge of local geography. When I confide that I am a teacher, we often converse on the subject of education. One said, "Americans are lucky. You can go to school almost free and you are even allowed to fail sometimes. In my country, if you fail one course out of five, you must repeat the whole term." I was reminded of a trigonometry class which I squeaked through only with massive support and tutoring and I thanked God for a "looser" system. Would I even be a teacher now if that standard had been applied?

Most of these cabbies, I learn, are either part or full-time students handling seventy-hour driving weeks along with academic courses which will qualify them for a degree that they will take back to their developing countries to improve them, or which will enable them to eventually bring the family here. They are strikingly similar in their aims to my Irish immigrant grandparents. I heard so many stories about the grandmother who was met at the railroad station in the late nineteenth century by one of her uncle's employees who asked, "Are you Cronin's greenhorn?" She was, and she later found another, also from Ireland. Together they settled down to raise a family, in the United States—ours. Her great-grandchildren have all gone to college and equipped themselves with the tools to be productive members of society. Four law degrees and one Ph.D. do not mean they are making millions in today's economy but it does insure their absence from welfare rolls. My cab drivers congratulate me on this and I think how ordinary it seems to us in a world where every American mother knows that her children have great potential, even if their educational debts are massive.

One "dark and stormy night" my driver told me that in his country a "woman like you" (presumably meaning gray-haired and sixty) would be perfectly safe on the streets even at 3:00 a.m. "Do you know what they would do to anyone who touched you?" I averred that I did not need to know and I swallowed my views of some practices of punishment common in his land in favor of a safe trip home. We went to more neutral subjects than crime in America and human rights abuse abroad. That I, a woman, might not have been allowed unescorted on his streets at 3:00 p.m. or 3:00 a.m. did not occur to him.

A scholarly African asked if he could leave his vocabulary tapes playing and wondered what I thought of his pronunciation. When I complimented him on it and left a book which had been sent to me by a publisher, he thanked me profusely and helped me across the somewhat icy sidewalk as though I were a queen. Projections of population experts inform us that by the century's end, one out of four Americans will be foreign-born or the child of a foreigner. That does not shock me as much as the news of my ancestors' arrival terrorized the nativists in the nineteenth century. Considering the cab drivers I've met in cabs and in my classes, they will be great additions to the "salad" of America. True, many of these new immigrants don't "melt" as well as my grandparents did. But flight from economic or religious persecution and privation ties the immigrant generations together. There really is not that much difference.

Shakespeare said it in the lines he gave Shylock, pleading for understanding in the courtroom: "If you prick us, do we not bleed? If you tickle us, do we not laugh? If you poison us, do we not die?"

To my dark-skinned cab driver, it did not matter that the children who died at Waco were mostly white. He said, "I have children and I can imagine how they suffered." If my own children feel as deeply about other human beings and their suffering, I will be proud.

XIII
Modern Woman

1988. A rough summer. I've been the facilitator. A person once told me that's what a teacher was and I almost hit her. Now I find myself that—and it's hard. G. K. Chesterton was right in saying a woman had to be a universalist. Judy Sykes says that's what a wife is.

You are at the mercy of the moods, needs, and pleasures of those around you. It's hard—hard—hard.

Maybe we just ought to "be there" for one another, but that is not what a facilitator is. It is much more. The term again occurred to me this summer. After a school year which seemed to go on interminably (the Lord intended there to be semesters, not quarters which extended into late June), I planned to catch up on household projects, read all the books I had not had time for, and generally enjoy a restful summer.

Naive me. In another context my husband (or as he likes to say "the Man I live with") once said, "Oh Mary Jane, don't be so naive." Once in a while he could be right. The "summer help" home from college had landed jobs starting at three different hours in the early A.M. I ran a shuttle service back and forth to the train, attributing my sacrifice to the peace of mind it brought me knowing that if they walked they would barely (if at all) leave themselves enough time to cross the tracks before boarding the train. My worst scenario saw all those well-educated brains (with loans not paid) sprayed across the intersection. Could I lie in bed? And so, I drove them. And drove them. And drove them.

Then came the visitors. The best lodgings are those belonging to your roommate's family. There were four sets of these, and each one needed street guides, road maps, train schedules, sandwiches for lunch, and finally the inevitable ride to the airport. One son even said, "Nice driving, Mom."

Was it fun? You bet! Was it chaos? Of course! No one complained that as we remodeled, the only working shower was in the basement. What matter if the fixtures from the other bathroom, the one being tiled, were in the middle of the kitchen floor? It may not have helped the aesthetic scene to have a toilet next to the refrigerator, but at least no one made the mistake of using it there, the subject of a not inconsiderable nightmare.

Each one of the four sets of roommates departed with a cheery "It was great Mrs. Kearney. Remember, if you're ever passing through Poughkeepsie (Laredo, Sault Ste. Marie, wherever), be sure to stay with us."

Finally, it was my summer. So, I settled down to enjoy what was left. One day I was checking the spelling of a word in the unabridged dictionary and I saw the word "facilitator—one who makes easy the work of others." That's what I had been. My eyes grew dim. That hated word. I considered forgoing my "facilitations" but I thought I would be written off as a whiner. Then I recalled G. K. Chesterton in a kinder age called a facilitator simply "one who cared." Not bad, I thought. Even a modern woman should want to be called caring.

XIV
CHILDHOOD AND TV'S REAL VIOLENCE: THE END OF CONVERSATION

I've heard a lot about eras ending in 1984, all the way from Orwell's portrayal of the death of freedom to the TV critics' straight-faced assertion that the light-hearted satires called "sit-coms" are headed for a demise. What seems not to have occurred to the era-enders is that Orwell's was a warning, not a prediction, and the situation comedies are not so comedic now that the situations are so common. But the announcement that brought me to my feet and reminded me of time's passing was the simple notice within the last few weeks that Captain Kangaroo was going off the air—retiring—forever!

Now my era of young motherhood (was I really ever young?) was the Captain Kangaroo period. With all due appreciation for Mr. Rogers who is always nice but sometimes oh-so-boring and for Sesame Street which is never dull but sometimes an assault upon the senses, I'll stick with Captain Kangaroo. His understated sophistication and ability to laugh with us, at ourselves, were the ultimate kindness to the parents who had that benighted idea that the television set was not where you sent the kids but what you watched with them. Mr. Greenjeans was unadulterated corn and Bunny Rabbit undiluted spoof, but always there was the Captain—erudite, sometimes gullible, but ever human.

I wanted to believe—and did—that Mr. Moose was the descendant of Eeyore in "Winnie the Pooh." We had a good laugh on Captain when the ping pong balls came down no matter what his avoidance technique was that day. Then, there were stories: "Stone Soup" came up at least once a year and the others ranged all the way from "Pin the duck on the Yangtze River" to the more adventurous Curious George. But always there was conversation, which had as its basis a respect for the other individual—be he four or forty. Thus, I wasn't surprised to hear Bob Keeshan, also Captain Kangaroo, sometime

14~ Childhood & TV's Real Violence: The End of Conversation

within the last year on a WBBM show about young people. Keeshan always encouraged parents to talk to, as well as of, their youngsters. I thought of the many shared laughs we had had about whether Bunny Rabbit would finally outwit Captain. Foolish they were, but they led to other things, and we were having a fine conversation.

As the years progressed, my five youngsters were out of the Captain's "audience age" and I was back teaching prospective teachers. My word to them was always "talk to the kids." One of my older students recently remarked to me that the greatest violence TV had ever done was not its reflection of violence itself but its elimination of conversation. She remembered all that she had learned as a child from overheard reminiscences of her elders—some of it not altogether complimentary to their ancestors. And she mourned its loss.

So this year, 1984, I'd like to add my voice to those of the ubiquitous "Trekkies" and the current Star Wars aficionados. I'd like to speak out for the Captain's people and even more so for their mellowing parents, those of us who were the lovers of Pooh and the sad-eyed Eeyore. Where are you, Mr. Greenjeans and Bunny Rabbit—who must be ever so hoary by now. Please don't disappear completely because there might be some geriatric "Kangaroos" who'd need a therapy session occasionally. They might even like a bump on the head—with a ping pong ball, of course.

XV
St. Valentine Knew We Needed Him

"We need a little Christmas—now" was a theme as well as a popular song from the musical based on Patrick Dennis's play *Auntie Mame*. As I recall, Mame had just been dismissed from her sales job for incompetence, when she returned home to her "poor soul" friend Agnes Gooch and an orphaned nephew who would now be her ward. With poverty seemingly her lot, and people depending upon her for emotional as well as financial support, she stages an infectiously buoyant scene of which that song is the background. While they decorate the Christmas tree early, the words remind them that though Christmas is an expression of the spirit, the ornaments and holly don't hurt.

Now, when all the decorations are packed away except for a straggly piece of evergreen behind the garbage can, we need a bit of that spirit. Though many of us mouth such things as "It's nice to have the house back to normal," we know how drab it all looks. In our hearts, we don't like to have our rationale for camaraderie and our excuse for frivolity packed away.

So we have elevated St. Valentine's Day to a position next only to Mother's Day and Christmas (ask the florists in case you doubt that). Old St. Valentine, bishop that he may have been in 270 A.D. and patron of loving hearts, never would have known the day named for him. One legend has it that he wrote notes of encouragement to folks, and those letters turned to gold. On that legend, the Middle Ages adopted him as the patron of lovers. Well, I say, whoever he was, we need him and use him well now.

It's the one holiday we all can embrace. My father, who eschewed birthdays and confined his Christmas observance to trimming our fresh balsam so much that we once had to purchase another, loved Valentine's Day. It was a day when he invariably treated my mother to "the best lookin' plant he could find for the best lookin' woman he

15 ~ St. Valentine Knew We Needed Him

had found!" It was his way of saying "you're great; life is rough now with kids sick and tempers short, but you make my life nicer every day." As a little girl, I often got a candy box heart from this same man who dealt in concrete blocks and stationary laundry tubs during his working hours. Valentine's Day was an excuse for him to be a bit sentimental.

Just a few years ago, comic Valentines were very popular. The snide "Roses are Red, Violets are Blue, the weather is cold and so are you" kind of verse was everywhere on the card shelves. Many of them went far beyond the Horatian kind of light-hearted satire to the nastier Juvenalian mode. Not so any more! As an inveterate Valentine shopper, I've noticed an almost complete about-face on the racks. For every one containing a not-so-funny dig, there are a dozen full of sweetness, replete with an implicit, if not direct, "you're O.K." or a whole lot more.

I'd like to argue that this reflects a greater sensitivity in our everyday contacts and maybe it does. The fact that we are incensed in our world of plenty that there are starved babies lying beside the road in Ethiopia and shocked to hear of children suffering from the abuse of parents and caretakers who ought to be their defenders might indicate this.

And, the fact that we often can't do anything directly about the just-mentioned crimes may rouse us to a greater sense of our attainable opportunities as well as our limitations. We need to tell those whom we can affect that we like them, love them, or maybe just approve of them. It need not be someone we want to spend our life with, but it shouldn't be just somebody we have to remember. It could be the school janitor or the mailman, the miserable woman at work who looks at her watch when we get back from lunch late, or the guy who sells us our newspaper.

Whoever it is that needs a Valentine, send it. I am not advocating the proliferation of gift-giving holidays. Indeed, I think we have too many of them, thanks to the merchants of America. I don't think we need "Sweetest Day" or "Grandparents' Day" to remind us to remember those in that category. But Valentine's Day is different. It appeals to the heart, its symbol, but it stimulates the creative imagination. I don't know if he knew about Christmas bills and taxes, but the Valentine Saint sure knew that there are times when "we need a little Christmas now."

XVI
The Art of the Unfinished

Upon the advent of No. 2 child and No. 1 son—and ever since—I never finish anything. Of all the adjustments required in marriage, this was surely the most difficult. For a while—about four years to be exact—dinner was late, kids' bedtime was late, and it took me all night to clean up after both. The evening ended with the house relatively straight and no time at all left for us just to be together.

After all I had to finish. It never occurred to me that time which had belonged to me just wasn't mine anymore. When I was teaching, I could sit up doing those papers or preparing that class and go to school red-eyed next day and it was my own business. Even with one little one, I could cut a corner here and there. But when that little girl was followed by four brothers within the first eight years of married life, there just wasn't time for anything.

My husband could foresee twenty years of evenings spent madly pursuing the monstrous goal I had created—being finished! When we finally looked at our problem, we decided that there was much more in life for us than that. Our chance or providential or call-it-what-you-will meeting in the research library was surely not for this. We began to carefully cultivate the art of the "unfinished."

Now if I were to determine to finish that closet shelf before dinner or get that last piece of folded clothing put away, I would need at least forty-eight hours in the day. While I pursued my sense of accomplishment, the baby would have started to scream because I didn't have time to feed him his mashed potatoes before we all sat down; the school kids would have come in from outside play and begun a project on the would-be dinner table; and the toddler would be sitting in the kitchen whimpering because his bread-basket says it's time to eat.

Now my sense of accomplishment is measured in things that would bring a smirk to the efficiency expert's face. One-third of a basket of clothes folded and I'm elated! The salad materials washed and into the refrigerator without ambush and I am triumphant! When the table remains set without an eighteen-month old resetting it according to his own sense of order, I feel life is good.

Meanwhile we've started one of our ever-continuing stories about Ella and Rex. (They are the twin children of Cinderella and the prince who arrived in our family when our daughter demanded that her favorite fairy tale not end.) We have administered three Band-Aids and four kisses and refereed an intramural fight.

Though nothing is finished, we eat at a decent time and the children are dispatched to bed, if not all bathed, then at least partly washed. Then we have that precious few minutes to laugh over the day's events and wonder together what we'll do about them.

We bought a big old house not long ago and I think we were looking for a place which would provide room to get away from the unfinished. When my husband says, "Come on into the living room and leave that stuff for another time," I know he approves of my cultivation of the art of the unfinished. We both know that the day will come when all things will be in place and we will sit down at night with our jobs finished. Our aim is to make sure we aren't finished first.

XVII
The Back to School Party

Teachers ourselves, my husband and I were very concerned that starting back to school be an important event in our family. Rather than have an end-of-the-school-year celebration, we inaugurated a back to school party to be held just before school opened each year. Some new things had to be purchased anyway, so we just added a something special that each one wanted every year, wrapped them up, and made it a celebration. As colleges started earlier and new jobs summoned just after mid-summer, we had to vary the date but "party" we did.

As the years went on and people got some humorous perspective on themselves, my husband and I had awards as a "take-off" on honors-assembly certificates. They would be for "a growing expertise in deferring trash emptying until it reached the level of a refined skill" and such things as that. One son, a classics major, always received his in Latin, some of it "pig variety" when we were lost for a word.

This year, four of our five children will be here, and the fifth, our daughter who teaches legal writing in Vermont, will be on the phone hook-up. While sending her some special clothes that she wanted recently, I found in her bedroom drawer all of her certificates, neatly piled. They were for such things as "a sense of creative cookery which renders pots permanently blackened and palates temporarily."

They seem to like the party so well that one is flying back from a vacation early to be there, and everybody is still in school one way or another. All families should nurture traditions, and traditions that celebrate education should rank very high indeed.

XVIII
Prototype Letter to an Independent Young Adult Away in College

I'm glad to see you doing so well in your college milieu. I won't call them college living quarters because the noise of stereos, young men's falsetto yells, and banging of doors to showers can hardly be called that. Was it for this that we kept the house quiet for years depriving ourselves sometimes of a favorite program so that you could study? I know you said you go to the library, but still . . . .

I'm glad we kept the telephone lines open and free that first year. That way I knew when the peanut butter cookies and an encouraging letter were sorely needed. I have heard it said that future generations will not have letters and papers of famous people to publish because they didn't write any. I'll have a few of yours: "Dear Mom—I'm going to flunk that test tomorrow. Send cookies." Or "I got my French quiz back. It was O.K.—Thanks for cookies—send more."

I'm glad you have strong views, but I hope you lose some—but not all—of that blessed certainty of youth about world politics, peoples' actions, and your siblings' faults. As for me, I gave up some of those judgments about the time I became a parent. I think. In the meantime, be the best possible person you can be. Remember that though you have emerged from childhood, we haven't outgrown parenthood.

Last week, I watched the robins in their nest on the drainpipe next door. One day, there were little beaks reaching skyward for food dropped by Pa and Ma. The next day it was a flying lesson and then they were gone. It's not so easy for us humans.

Love, Mom

The phone you say? What's that? Prayers for a history test on Tuesday? MORE peanut butter cookies? Oh, these I.Y.A.'s.

XIX
Thoughts on Delivering a Son— To College

Having successfully delivered my fifth child/fourth son to college this year, I joined that vast army of parents who serve by waiting for news of their I.Y.A.'s (Independent Young Adults).

We all know that in late summer, kids by the score troop off to school, taking with them any presentable bath towels, the only clock radio in the house that works, and Dad's razor. They leave behind them caches of half-worn tennis shoes, numerous souvenirs of high school triumphs, and miscellaneous parents in varying states of bankruptcy, sadness, and exhaustion.

My medicine for the malady was to write a letter. It read:

Dear Son:

I'm glad I'm sending you off to college and not to war, and I hope that you are turning 18 in a world which just might be coming to realize that such a conflict would be terminal to all humans, not just to young men in their prime.

I'm glad that we watched the brown rabbit eat breakfast in our yard this summer even though we watched him too long one morning and I ended up having to drive you to work.

I'm glad you took me to hear Harry Chapin perform a couple of years ago before you and your friends were old enough to drive. I found out that "All my life's a circle" just in time. Had I waited another year, beloved folk singer Harry would have been gone.

I'm sorry that I didn't go to a few of those far-out movies you invited me to. If your father and I went alone now, we'd probably be cited for vagrancy.

I'm sorry that we talked so much about heavy college expenses that when you got your college checking account you felt you had to ask us if we were short and needed a check from you. Most of all, I'm glad you're ours though not quite as much anymore.

Love, Mom

The phone you say? What's that? More gym socks, peanut butter cookies, a can opener, peanut butter cookies, your dog-eared dictionary . . . peanut butter cookies. We'll see what we can do next Sunday. Oh those I.Y.A.'s!

Love, Mom

(Reprinted from the *Chicago Sun-Times*)

XX
ON OUR NEED FOR SILENCE, OR RECONSIDERING HAMLET

The thoughts we keep in our heart of hearts—the ordinary everyday ones—are often fit to be told only to ourselves. The fact that we can do this, rather than being a symptom of mental illness, keeps us sane.

She was small and blond and about seven years old. I overheard her childish voice when I took out the junk which should have been emptied after the party last night. Bouncing a ball against the garage door, I heard her say, "I know I'll get yelled at for doing this. But sometimes I don't want to play dolls. Pretty soon, it'll go over in fussy Mrs. Johnson's flowers and then . . . ." Her voice trailed off and when I heard no response, I knew she was alone. My little neighbor was engaged in that quite perennial and time-honored pastime—talking to herself.

I thought of my own life and how often I had said, "Look, girl, you better break down and say you're sorry or do something nice for her before any more time passes." Some things have to be sorted out within oneself. Or, years ago, "I just don't want to go out with him any more. When he calls, I'll tell him we don't have common interests." Of course when he did call, what I said to him didn't come out quite that way at all, but I had made my decision by talking it over—with myself. That was my moment of truth—the only time I was totally honest was when I talked to myself alone.

Why do people talk to themselves? Because there are lots of things that are too personal—or too trivial—to say to others. When you've broken the only good dish you can use for a big casserole, or when you've waited for the mailman for the fifth day in a row in hopes of that special letter, whom are you going to tell about it? Some of us confide these things to a higher being, but I suspect that, wrongly

I'm sure, we retain the idea that He isn't that interested in our silliness. Sure, there are people with whom we just can't wait to share a funny story—even if it's on ourselves—or to whom we can say, "Wait till I tell you the dumb thing I did." But most of the time we tuck those things away until finally our mood of depression or habit of feeling sorry makes us say, "I have to give myself a good talking to."

Hamlet wasn't mad—or at least not yet—when he delivered his soliloquies. And though our society frowns upon it, we all do talk to ourselves. T. S. Eliot said in "The Love Song of J. Alfred Prufrock" that you "prepare a face to meet the faces that you meet." We all have to do a lot of that, but I for one like my little neighbor's solution. Do a bit of talking to yourself.

XXI
A Thoroughly Modern "Modest Proposal"

Recently, it was brought to my attention by a popular columnist of the women's pages that the presence of mothers shopping with children provides a "traffic hazard" in the supermarket to other customers (assuredly the columnist). She suggests that these mothers seeking to give their offspring "creative" experiences choose "off" hours when "the traffic is open to amateurs." (These "off hours" are evidently when the columnist is not shopping.)

Underlying the column is the assumption that the mother wants to shop with her children. Ask any woman who has had more than one toddler as her responsibility and she will tell you that the day when her husband is mercifully home with a cold becomes her shopping day. While the kiddies and their ailing father nap, then and only then does she find the experience bearable—let alone creative. Contrary to the writer's assumption, she does not enjoy the company of egg-crushing one-year olds and three-year-old kiddie-program watchers with all their "felt" needs. But shopping must be done, so she cheerfully steers the shopping cart between the Scylla of dignified ladies (like the columnist) and the Charybdis of succulent displays guaranteed to make an impulsive buyer out of anyone, especially a susceptible three-year old.

Regarding this problem of the children, a number of solutions have been suggested throughout the centuries. The most graphic one that I can recall was that "modest proposal" of Swift for relieving the English nobility of the burden of the poverty-racked Irish. Three hundred years have passed since Jonathan Swift was born and surely we have progressed beyond the infanticide he suggested—albeit his suggestion was satirical. Maybe we could provide a sort of pen-like structure next to the place where shopping carts are stored. A mother could check her toddlers in and they could be numbered like the carts. This should keep the matter well organized; it would not be necessary to stack the children. If there is any problem of the penned children nipping at the heels of departing shoppers, their mouths could be muzzled with wads of bubble gum, easily available at the checkout counter.

So much for a possible solution. It is easily seen that it is a long time since the columnist shopped with children. Perhaps she never did and maybe her mother before her called or sent a note to the friendly neighborhood grocer. He in turn bundled up her groceries and brought them up the back steps and into her kitchen where she unpacked them at leisure. Alas, the neighborhood grocer who fills and delivers your order is an institution not often found these days. The few pennies which he must charge per item over the supermarket price in order to survive have made it impossible for many to do so. Indeed in some neighborhoods, the neighborhood grocer does not exist.

So the majority of us will have to trundle our kids off to the supermarket when we shop. Last time I was there with my $89.43 order, the manager said he hoped I'd stop in anytime. I guess he didn't want me to confine my shopping to "off hours."

Still, the idea of checking and muzzling the young will prevail, no doubt, and in a society where the voice of the people is the bedrock principle, I must prepare to yield. I wonder—can I get my neighbor's used dog muzzle cheap?

XXII
Thoughts on Taking Down the Holiday Decorations

There's an implicit sadness in taking down the Christmas tree. My mother once commented that the absence of the tree, which had brightened the home during the holidays, suddenly made it look sparse and bare, almost like a lady who had to put aside her finery because the ball was over.

This year I have been slower than usual to remove all of the holiday "stuff" around the house. After a generally garrulous, sometimes hilarious, and only occasionally claustrophobic two weeks, most of our family have gone back to their own "digs"—dorms, apartments, sometimes I lose track. But I don't think that it's the "empty nest" syndrome which has slowed me down. No, I think it might have more to do with the pleasant reminiscences which I have had over the last few days. On this tree is the celluloid doll with the pushed-in face done by me lo these many years ago when my father and brother wouldn't let me help with the lights. At least, that's how I remember it. And there are the styrofoam snowmen with detergent-cap heads, far away from the doll of the '30s and out of a do-it-yourself era.

Next are the faded felt stockings, once beautiful before a basement flood—they were stitched years ago by a grandmother for children whose pictures had to be sewn on the front. (Is there a front on a stocking?) There is even a sequined one labeled "Misty"—simple but much more than that, as it is a reminder of the eleven-year period when our cat delighted and terrified us, finally using up all of her lives. They all lay there as I removed them, a mute reminder of what Keats was talking about in "Ode on a Grecian Urn," when he praised the ideal beauty pictured there, the melodies unheard and the bride unravished.

XXIII
SOME THOUGHTS ON MULTI-CULTURALISM AND CHILDREN'S READINGS

If Francis Bacon were writing today about the wealth of American children's multi-ethnic books, he would find many to be tasted with their dramatic and colorful illustrations, other great tales to be swallowed whole, and a few volumes, complete with fine art, worthy to be chewed and digested.

This was not always so. First of all, earlier Americans didn't "take much" to stories whose heroines were not blond, fair-skinned, and Anglo-Saxon—that dark exotic beauty was fine for the Arabian Nights, but not for the nineteenth and early-twentieth-century reading populace. Second, many families saw children as an economic factor most valuable when they were old enough to get jobs and contribute to the solvency of the unit. Children's books, which might prolong the period of "daydreams and idleness," were not important and, except for those with explicit moral instruction, were not purchased in great numbers.

Gradually, however, the idea that children are not just undersized adults but special people to be nurtured gained credence. Developmental psychology examined the effects of childhood experiences and the world of commerce discovered children as customers. Better-educated parents responded to the growing body of literature aimed directly at children and caused a minor boom in this area. At the same time in this late twentieth century, countries such as England, Canada, and America have experienced a considerable rise in their immigrant and refugee arrivals. That such newcomers do not melt but, like earlier pilgrims, retain much of their cultural identity is an acknowledged fact and one now encouraged in schools and communities.

Stories of what used to be called hyphenated Americans are sold along with those depicting Dick and Jane, and they are read by all children.

Sometimes in the recent past, though, as in Marie Hall Ets's *Bad Boy, Good Boy* (Crowell, 1967), the immigrant picture painted was horrendous. Here the Hispanic father puts the mother out of the house because she can't cook. She finally comes back, after receiving a pleading letter from her son which the staff of the day care center has helped him to write. She has been taught to cook by the white lady she works for and all is now harmonious. Terrible as that picture was, there are now many more positive multi-cultural images in stories like *The Most Beautiful Place in the World* by Ann Cameron (Knopf, 1988). Here seven-year-old Juan, supported by a strong grandmother, yearns for an education which he feels will bring him hope. He loves his town, "the most beautiful place in the world," and learns that one must speak up for something that he really wants badly—in this case, a chance to go to school.

Good and evil are contrasted in Roberts San Souci's *Talking Eggs* (Dial, 1989), which pits the good sister against the bad sister and mother in a Creole story set in Louisiana. It has a fairy-tale aura to it, fantastic animals, and attractive black characters drawn by Jerry Pinkney.

The need to belong is dramatized by a spunky little heroine in Bette Bao Lord's *In the Year of the Boar and Jackie Robinson* (Harper, 1984), where Bandit, or Shirley Temple Wong as she calls herself, arrives from China the same year that Jackie Robinson, first black man in major league baseball, is playing with the then-Brooklyn Dodgers. The alienation she suffers is amply balanced by a spirit of optimism, which Roni Natov, "Living in Two Cultures" (*The Lion and the Unicorn*, 1987), finds in contrast to the bewilderment felt by Maxine Hong Kingston who describes her childhood in *The Woman Warrior* (Knopf, 1976). Kingston calls her girlhood a struggle among ghosts. The old ghosts were all the fears and myths her people brought and the new ghosts were the totally unfamiliar patterns of the West.

But Shirley Wong knows she can make it in this country which her teacher says is a place where "each man . . . has the right to pursue his own happiness. For no matter what his race, religion or creed, be he pauper or president, he has the right to speak his mind . . . . To make a difference. To change what has been. To make a better America." At the end of the book, when her mother tells her she is "with expectant happiness," the little Chinese girl knows she will teach her new brother everything, not just about how to hit a home run and chew bubble gum but how to speak Chinese and how the sun sets over the Mountain of Ten Thousand Steps. She will help him love both cultures. They will belong.

Some might find this picture a simplistic view of the immigrant or minority American experience, but the affirmation in this book and many others gives children the same sense of power which Bruno Bettleheim cites in *The Uses of Enchantment* as the reason for the continued popularity of the folk fairy tales. The young and the weak and sometimes the simple can make a difference, these narratives say. Sometimes they need a little help from a magical figure, but who doesn't require a miracle occasionally? The initial action has to be theirs, and then they must cooperate with the force for good, wherever it comes from. A book showing the underdog gaining power is *The Adventures of High John the Conqueror* (Orchard, 1989) by Steve Sanfield. Here is a prototype of an unlikely hero who succeeds. Set in slave times, John's cleverness helps him outsmart the master and win freedom. He overcomes terrible conditions and discouraging odds to give the young reader a vicarious triumph.

Feeling connected to one's background and heritage is important too, and two beautiful books, *The Patchwork Quilt* by Valerie Flournoy (Dial, 1985) and *The Keeping Quilt* by Patricia Polacco (Simon and Schuster, 1988), both capture that linkage. The first depicts a strong black family cooperating to create a quilt which will represent some of the family's memories, and the second narrates the history of a quilt, brought all the way from Russia and used as a wedding tent, a coverlet, and a conveyor of tradition in this Jewish family.

These and many other recently written multi-cultural books are found in libraries and bookstores today. Their popularity and the enthusiastic support they enjoy from children, parents, teachers, and other interested observers bode well for the '90s. Children, like adults, want to see images of themselves reflected in literature, and the celebration in these volumes of diversity and the spirit is a measure of literature's ability to overcome narrowness and inhumanity.

XXIV
Cabbage Patch Mania Reveals Society Shift

At this Christmas season, the newspaper has carried daily pictures of long lines of frantic parents in quest of a homely, cuddlesome, unfashionable doll—the Cabbage Patch doll. These unlikely creatures are the subject of a craze as startling when it surfaced a year ago as that of the pet rock or the mood ring a few seasons earlier.

Indeed, a scheme to sell fake Cabbage Patch dolls enraged the populace recently and led to all kinds of alarm about the materials used in these dolls as well as their authenticity. Parents who had gotten up at 4 a.m. to stand outside a store that was scheduled to get a shipment of these scarce items were not happy to think that their sizable investment of money and time might have been devoted to something not genuine.

At any rate, this newest national love could reflect a deeply felt desire in our society not answered by the robots and self-propelled airplanes, the computer games and the laser guns—i.e., a need to be needed.

True, little girls (and now even little boys, mercifully) have always loved dolls. "By dee" dolls were popular in the '30s. They drank water and wet the same. They were followed by a series of moving, talking, singing life-size prototypes of real babies and children culminating in the Barbie dolls of the late '50s, '60s, and '70s. But these supposedly orphaned moppets known as Cabbage Patch dolls are the rejects of society, and they are different.

Barbie, modeled after the chic American teenager, but more svelte than most teens glimpsed at the local shopping mall, was, well, perfect. She had a smooth hairstyle, a wardrobe ranging from jumpsuits to evening gowns. She had perfect teeth, perfect legs, and a perfect boyfriend—Ken. She was the ultimate, we thought.

Her sunglasses and sports car took her through her perfect day, and she returned to her perfect house with its ruffled boudoir and perfect kitchen. She was around for a long time and we never worried that she would be rejected by the college of her choice, be tossed over by her boyfriend, or have her job eliminated in a budget cut. Hers was the perfect world to inherit. But the world turned out not to be perfect. We found that it harbored war and death on one side and looked away to see pollution and corruption, even at the heart of government, on the other.

So enter upon the scene the floppy, uncoordinated bit of imaginative design—the Cabbage Patch creature—and we see something different. We see someone looking for a home and someone who comes complete with adoption papers, waiting for some small person to say, "I will be responsible for you . . . . I love you." All kinds of messages could be read and I suspect will be drawn from this, but I'd like to suggest just one. We all need someone to need us, and the Cabbage Patch dolls do—desperately. We can't do a great deal, individually, about the problems of our world—nuclear war, famine, acid rain—but we certainly can provide for a little creature who looks to us like it needs to be picked up and hugged, taken to bed, and loved some more.

Within the past year the centennial of Pinnochio was celebrated—the winsome, long-nosed kid made by Papa Gepetto who was adopted and loved even when he wasn't deserving of it. Finally, though, to become real he had to sacrifice and I wonder if that's what some of the kids are responding to—a love that requires sacrifice. The end of the era of instant gratification may be symbolized by this homely but winsome-looking creature that might have been found in a cabbage patch.

So, goodbye, Barbie. Hello, Cabbage Patch. Not such a bad way to ring out 1984 that had such dire predictions attached to its passing.

(Reprinted from the *Chicago Sun-Times*)

XXV
Broken Wrist a Real Ice-Breaker

I long ago found that walking a baby or a dog in Chicago is the equivalent of an invitation to conversation. Now, as the result of an accident, I have discovered a third such opening.

Having shattered my wrist during the only two hours of ice that Chicago had in December, I reconciled myself to two months in plaster and sling while planning strategies for carrying out my usual roles—homemaker and English teacher.

A broken arm a while back had prepared me, I thought, for the restrictions. But that had been my left arm, and this was my right! This was my writing, speaking, filing arm. This was the appendage with which I ate, combed, carried, caressed, collected, and charged at the department store. What was I to do? I confess that a basic principle of my life has been that of Tennessee Williams's Blanche in *A Streetcar Named Desire*, "I have always depended on the kindness of strangers." I have found these are words to live by. But there are limits!

I tried various strategies. A large Field's shopping bag brought clothes upstairs from the dryer in the basement. A bed of potholders enabled me to remove a roast from the oven with one hand and set it on the kitchen floor until someone arrived home—just as long as I learned to lock the cat up first. My handy eighty-year-old mother-in-law enlarged blouse sleeves to accommodate my shoulder-to-palm cast, and a manual typewriter on the kitchen counter enabled me to peck out messages to children doing the shopping and students whose papers I was correcting. Using parts of my body I had scarcely noticed before, I was partially back in business.

Once sprung from the house, I found that my very visible and seemingly temporary infirmity brought me a harvest of advice and counsel from people formerly mute when I passed them in the cafeteria or the ladies' room.

One day when my tray-carrying colleagues had to go elsewhere and I went alone to the lunch counter in the Mid-Continental Plaza, I met the most amazing lady of my plaster-bound experience. She drove up in her motorized wheelchair, laboriously hoisted herself to the counter seat, and ordered lunch. When she asked me to pass the cream pot, we began to converse.

She came to work, I learned, in a van provided for handicapped people, kept her own apartment, and managed "just fine" to do office work and handle accounts. But she had to keep her head down as she ate, handled her utensils with difficulty, and generally showed signs of a central nervous system disorder. When she got herself back into her transporting chair, she wished me a happy and prosperous return to full use of my arm and rode off. The irony of her "full use" wish either didn't strike her or—more likely—she found it irrelevant.

What I did learn is that people with a limitation will go to extreme, seemingly bizarre lengths to "do it themselves," even if it takes them ten times the effort and quadruple the length of time. They need to see that they can feed, clothe, and transport themselves in all but emergencies. They need to go to bed exhausted at the end of a day, not because they have been unable to participate or accomplish goals but because they have been part of the struggle to make it.

Never again will I chuckle, as I did last fall, when I hear someone make a crack about curbless sidewalks for wheelchairs. But I hope we will soon hear from the inventors about how one-handed people can tie up a plastic garbage bag, open a tightly sealed jar, or pull up support pantyhose before the delivery man stops ringing the doorbell and leaves the front porch. That last one takes some real creativity.

(Reprinted from the *Chicago Sun-Times*)

XXVI
Mom and Pop Robin—The Ideal Summer Visitors

Our summer residents have just left. They did not add to the local economy or drain the natural resources or consume parking space with their vehicles. On the other hand, their comings and goings were duly appreciated by neighbors who never bother them with an invitation to a patio party.

They are the robins that arrive each year, building their nest in the elbow of the drain pipe next door within easy visual range of our favorite reading spot.

I'm not even positive they are the same robins that came last year, but they bear a family resemblance.

One could learn quite a bit about recycling from their diligent use of available materials. Pop and Mom arrived early to collect sticks, small pieces of vegetation, and lubricated leaves left from the long winter's soaking. Once I even saw a red paper ribbon escaped from our trash festooning their nest. Having built a residence, they lay eggs, and brooding time begins. Dad brings Mom choice tidbits and she sits ever so carefully, keeping her future family warm.

One day we see little heads rising above the edge of the nest and an incredible rushing back and forth with food. Both Mom and Pop always seem to be depositing a worm, a seed, or a piece of berry into open, uplifted beaks.

To say that the baby birds gobble up these morsels is an understatement. Their parents must be worn to the feather, so hungry are these young-uns.

Such dedicated parenting is a sight to behold. Daily the babies grow and daily they are watched. One got too close to the edge of the nest one day and got a smart knock from Mom. Wing exercises are a daily routine in preparation for the moment of departure.

This rite of passage must be the veritable "trying one's wings." Mom and Dad got them down to the top of our fence; three flew off soon but a fourth didn't make it. Mom didn't know our family was taking turns keeping close guard against cats or squirrels, so she stayed on the nearby fence, darting down quarter-hourly to scold and prod. Finally, this little bird soared. We restrained our cheers so as not to frighten Mom.

The parents did not return this season to the nest. Maybe there will be a new nest in its place. I hope Mom and Dad will rendezvous in Georgia or some such spot since dedicated parenting deserves a reward.

Am I still talking about the robins? Say, have any of the kids, or rather Independent Young Adults, called today? I guess I was distracted for a moment or so. For the birds, it's so much easier. From a distance, at least, it looks that way.

(Reprinted from the *Chicago Sun-Times*)

XXVII
No Wonder Many Teachers-to-Be Fall Short

In the last few weeks statistics about prospective teachers have been released, accompanied by appropriate clucks and cries of "Can you imagine?" The scholastic aptitude of young people studying to be teachers, according to the figures, is lower than that of the general college population.

For those of us in the profession, that's no surprise.

The prestige of teaching has eroded steadily as the world has discovered that girls can do higher math and master scientific concepts quite well—so long as their parents and teachers don't tell them too early that they are frivolous, frothy creatures. Not surprisingly, they have been making their way into architecture and engineering, accounting and astrophysics.

At the same time, we are told that not only can't many Johnny's read, but they also can't write. As a matter of fact, neither can their teachers. This was illustrated in a recent TV report on Channel 2 that showed teachers' misspelled assignments on a classroom blackboard and semi-literate notes to parents. And now we have the scores to prove it!

What has happened is this: while other fields have been opening up, teaching—still dominated numerically by women, at least on the primary and secondary level—has not emphasized the skill and intelligence, as well as creativity, required of a prospective teacher. Too many teacher-preparation programs no longer emphasize the old two-pronged fork of a liberal education—a body of knowledge, including history of civilizations, literature, philosophy, and the arts, and the mental discipline that comes with the study of mathematics, science, and logic.

The best way to discourage poor students from following a career they cannot handle is to challenge them while in college. They soon will discover that loving children is not enough and, one hopes, find another career.

I recently participated in a radio interview show because the small teachers college where I work was celebrating ten years of offering programs to urban students.

While all the guests to be "hyped" were sitting around a table drinking coffee before air time, someone mentioned that I was engaged in the education of teachers. Four other people were there. One had just bought a once-great Chicago restaurant that had gone into decline. Another was a successful young black actor. A third was a guitarist who had introduced some new version of rock. The fourth was the interviewer. Everyone suddenly felt compelled to tell the story of a teacher he remembered—ranging from a third-grade harridan in Peoria to a gentle high school drama coach who said, "You have what it takes." Though we were discussing education, not one of these successful, dynamic people wanted to tell us what was the matter with the profession—but all had to speak about teachers they had found unforgettable.

It brought back a lesson I learned as a young high school teacher 30 years ago. A girl had given me a terrible hassle while we read and discussed *Macbeth*, and I was surprised to see her at my desk one afternoon after classes. Following some small talk, she sputtered out: "Why are you here? I bet you could have been a reporter or a personnel manager or [and here she surveyed my figure very critically] maybe even an airline stewardess. Why are you here, with us?"

She was not being fresh; she really wanted to know. When I recounted the incident to an old and seasoned colleague later, she mused, "Your lesson from that, my dear, is that most of all they are studying you."

I thought of that when I read those statistics the other day. In 1952, when I graduated from college, as in 1902, there were not many opportunities elsewhere. So, many very good students looking for a challenge went into teaching. Now there is much to lure the best and brightest.

Let's offer a real challenge to those who even consider such a demanding profession as teaching. Let's make it hard for them. Let's remind them that somewhere in their background, as was the case with those people on that radio show, there was a Mr. Chips or even a Miss Brodie who prodded them on.

(Reprinted from the *Chicago Sun-Times*)

XXVIII
Some Things in Life—And at Notre Dame—Keep Repeating

When our youngest son graduates Sunday from the University of Notre Dame Law School, we will be completing a family odyssey to South Bend which began in 1979. Four graduations later, we return once again.

One time long ago while visiting a prestigious midwestern university with our eldest son, then in his senior year of high school, I commented positively on its lovely campus. This quiet but determined 17-year-old looked me squarely in the eye and said, "Notre Dame has a beautiful campus, too, and that is where I want to go."

It was an "in-your-face" answer and left me gasping for breath. Getting into Notre Dame was a daunting task for someone living where we do. They sell N.D. sweatshirts in the local department stores and it is quite common to meet another person wearing one at church, the park, or the market. To many Chicagoans, Notre Dame is as much the home team as are the Chicago White Sox.

A quiet boy who was in the top level of his class, this son needed an inspiration. He found it soon afterward at a concert by Harry Chapin, folk singer and composer. I was sent along to the concert by my husband as a sort of chaperon to the fairly new driver and his three brothers. I still remember the smoke-filled balcony where I sat hearing Chapin croon:

All my life's a circle,
sunrise and sundown
The moon rolls through the nighttime
till the daybreak comes around.

28 ~ Some Things in Life—& at Notre Dame—Keep Repeating

In my son's college application essay, he referred to Chapin's theme of coming back. He recalled being taken to a Notre Dame football game at age ten and knowing even then that this was his place.

Chapin's words:

> *Seems like I've been here before,*
> *I can't remember when.*
> *But I got this funny feeling*
> *that we'll all be together again.*

Those words seemed written for our son. We always thought Chapin got our son into Notre Dame. We added the musician's name to the family prayer list when he was killed on a New York freeway a few years later.

So began the Notre Dame years, with our son's sister joining him there his junior year to attend law school.

There in the unique atmosphere of early Salvation Army discards which decorate Notre Dame dorm rooms, No. 1 son—as his father, mimicking Charlie Chan, called him—grew in wisdom and age and found a vocation while working with disabled kids on Saturdays.

When, five years later, the youngest brother was accepted into the university, I packed him off with confidence that he too would find people of purpose and humor and warmth. I admit that I was a bit disappointed when, calling him a few weeks into the school year on his 18th birthday, I got no answer.

Finally, at 11 p.m., the phone rang and an enthusiastic young man breathed, "Mom, you'll never guess whom I met at the Grotto tonight." And, not waiting for an answer: "Father Hesburgh! I told him it was my birthday. Don't you think that's a good omen?"

I did indeed and proceeded to chuckle over the incident. In the time that followed, I saw another brother, out in the business world for several years, go back to law school in the shadow of the Dome. He found a wife there as well as a degree.

When the youngest son—the one who had thought Father Hesburgh's wishes a "good omen"—decided to return to Notre Dame for a law degree, I knew we were entwined in this circle for good.

As we watch our youngest son receive that degree this Sunday, visions of fifteen years of Notre Dame education will dominate our memories. There he and all of us vicariously made friends, helped disabled kids, played Bookstore Basketball, and went to 11 p.m. Mass in Dillon Hall.

And when our caravan rolls away from campus that night—complete with our children's 92-year-old grandmother, who prayed this son through every set of exams, and with this son's 2-year-old niece, whose own tests lie in the future—we'll feel as Chapin did. Life is, indeed, a circle.

And we'll know with the certainty born of beloved repetition and remembered joy that:

> *Seems like I've been here before,*
> *I can't remember when.*
> *But I got this funny feeling*
> *that we'll all be together again.*

(Reprinted from the *South Bend Tribune*)

XXIX
AT LEAST TEN REASONS FOR THE TIRED TEACHER TO ANSWER THE SCHOOL BELL

Mary Jane's love of teaching and her commitment grew over the years. On January 29, 1994, she wrote, "I have decided to jot down a little as often as I can, since, after motherhood, this is where my heart is. Actually, without students to share something with, cut out an article for, I feel bereft. Does that reveal a lack of friends or interested family? I don't think so. We all need to feel we are building for the future—if not ours, then that of our grandchildren or students."

Her students' accolades over the years leave no doubt that Mary Jane was a rare and superb teacher. Here are some of her reflections on her craft. These are culled from unpolished notes for a talk she gave to several in-service teachers' programs.

This is my thirty-fifth return to the classroom. In our youth-conscious culture or society maybe people wouldn't want to hear from someone who has done it so long. We all know that does not necessarily mean he or she does it better. But let me try to itemize some of the things that bring me back each September with a sense of expectancy. When that goes, I'll have to find some other way or retire. Thus far, I see no signs.

As I set out to list the good things, I am reminded of that wonderful children's book of Judith Viorst, *The Tenth Good Thing About Barney*. In that book a little boy's cat has died and the boy is disconsolate. He doesn't want to eat his chicken or even his chocolate pudding. His mother says that they can have a funeral the next day and he should think of ten good things to say about Barney. The boy remembered that Barney was brave and smart and funny and clean and cuddly and handsome—that he only once ate a bird—that it was sweet when he purred in the little boy's ear and wonderful when he slept on his belly and kept him warm. When that amounted to only nine his mother told him to think about it.

The boy's next-door neighbor Annie says Barney is in heaven, and he says "no," Barney is in the ground. Later when his father is working outside and gets a packet of seeds to complete his gardening, and the boy tells the father he doesn't see any flowers there, the father tells him things change in the ground and this will give the seeds a place to live and then they will grow leaves and flowers. Then the boy asks if Barney will help them grow. That, he decides, is the tenth thing. He helps things grow. As with Barney, so with teachers.

As I continued along, other books kept popping into my mind. So I guess you might say I'm working up ten good things about teaching. There's that wonderful scene in *Macbeth* where the drunken porter is awakened on the night of the king's murder by those who had found the body and he thinks he is guarding the gates of hell. He has many people he puts down there—and I'm surprised one of them isn't a teacher. So the first good reason for staying in teaching—for better or worse you make your mark.

Another good thing about teaching is that you are helping people to greater independence—whether you are teaching them the first skills of decoding as you do in kindergarten or first grade or how to approach a research topic as you do and I do. Remember that moment in the *Narrative of Frederick Douglass*—a man who was a slave and eventually became a leader in the abolitionist movement—where he learns to read, and the transformation that reading brings to his life.

A third good reason is that you are constantly learning. That's not so in all jobs. I started to make a list last year of everything I had learned and gave up in fatigue. I learned from my students about Asian languages, that they don't have hard endings. I learned that people you would tell to write could not always do it when they came in cold, so you had to devise ways to warm them up. Of course maybe what you learned is that you never want to teach eighth-grade boys—or girls—again. I don't know if I can help you on that. When you plant a seed, you can usually tell what's going to happen. A plant is either going to make it in a short while or not. But you don't know that in teaching. The plant may sprout years hence.

A fourth thing about teaching is that we get to start over every September. Now far from being a negative factor, that's a plus. A friend of mine is a lawyer for the ACLU; she tells me that when her children were small they used to ask her how long she had to practice law before she got it right. Sometimes I wonder how long we'll have to practice before we get the magic formula. I don't think we will ever get it and that's where our creativeness comes in. We all know that the same thing doesn't work for everyone. I had a woman last year who said she was so desperate for ways to get the kids reading that she used to have seventh-grade boys give book reports by telling what was the matter with the book. She found that soon they were talking to each other about those books. And exchanging books. Some of them will end up hearing about a book which a friend hated but sounded pretty good to them. It was where I heard about *A Wrinkle in Time* and its various sequels by Madeleine L'Engle.

The flip side of that difficult class story and a fifth good thing about teaching is that a problem—even a problem class—does not last forever. One has to be optimistic in that way. I'm an optimist married to a pessimist. He has a codicil to add to Murphy's Law—you know, the one that says, "If anything can go wrong, it will." Well his addendum says Murphy was an optimist. But if you're not an optimist about the human condition, why teach?

Sixth, we get to try new things without "failing." I have done some horrendous things in my time. Usually the students will let you know if an assignment is too outrageous. Right now I'm trying journals or letters. I have them read a few journal-type things. One of the books I like which uses a journal as its base is *A Gathering of Days*, a Newbery-award-winning book. One time with a group of students I had them answer letters that immigrants wrote to the *Bintel Brief* compilation that comes from *The Jewish Daily Forward*. Immigrants would write with problems like: Should I marry the man my parents chose for me in the Old Country or the nice young medical student I have fallen in love with here—whom I am going to have to support through medical school? What do you think they answered? Another time I had a group of new Americans who had heard about Ann Landers. I photocopied Ann Landers's column without the answers; they wrote their own and then discussed why she answered as she did. Once they built up trust, we had a lot of fun and sharing.

Seventh, it's the greatest excuse to read or travel. I visited a friend last week in her seventies. She has now retired from active college teaching—except adult education stuff for which she has people waiting in line. But when I first knew her she was a busy woman teaching high school, living in a community of religious sisters, taking care of a big student organization, going to grad school, and writing articles. Now she's seventy-five and she's just as vibrant, just out with a new book chosen by a book club as its offering. She's going to Rome today to research her next book.

Recently, a lot of attention has been paid to an item called cultural literacy. I have to put it in my terms, as I do with the prime rate. I finally thought I would please my husband by learning what the prime rate is—the rate at which the banks lend money to Sears Roebuck. Whether it's the prime rate or prime beef, I know of no better way to become culturally literate than by reading. And, no doubt, travel is a very close second. Cultural literacy, or lack of it, according to E. D. Hirsch, is the basic information we need to thrive in the modern world. I notice students do not catch allusions such as those to Dante, Shakespeare, Henry Clay, Magellan, Job. "But," you say, "do they know Moamar Khadafi, Malcolm X, Richard Secord, Oliver North, Bruce Springsteen, and Madonna?" They may not be your favorite allusions, but build on them. When you say William Perry, you may mean the current Secretary of Defense while they are referring to someone called "Refrigerator," but that's good for a laugh anyway.

We were lucky our mothers read Grimm and Robert Louis Stevenson. On our own we perused Nancy Drew and the Rover Boys, all the books of the Oz series. We had teachers read us *The Five Little Peppers and How They Grew* in fifth grade while we waited to go home for the lunch bell. I had one college teacher whom we called the "Name Dropper," but I learned from him what it must have been like to have lived in early-twentieth-century England. He claimed to have had drinks with all the authors we read—Gerard Manley Hopkins, Evelyn Waugh, or Graham Greene. But he was part of my acculturation. I listened to my parents talk of Dillinger and Jelly Roll Morton and went to Maxwell Street. I heard from them of World

War I and the Battle of Belleau Wood where so many Americans died. The great flu epidemic of 1918 was a real event because an uncle had died in it, and the Depression was something that I remember. I bought *No Promises in the Wind*, Irene Hunt's book, for my son when he was thirteen to let him know what the Great Depression was.

Though students of today don't know these characters, I find them surprisingly eager to learn that Dumb Dora was the wife of David Copperfield, that Thor was not originally a cartoon in the newspaper, and that Ajax didn't start out as a cleaner. As a matter of fact, it's the only job I know of where you use, at one time or another, every scrap of knowledge, every technique, every trick you have learned. In doing so you will expand your own allusions, start to build on theirs, and you'll both be enriched.

The eighth good thing about teaching is that we get to use our own individuality. I think that's something you should point out to kids—in a light sort of way. We aren't clones, thank God, and the feeling that teachers should fit into a certain pre-disposed mold is nonsense. Kids are great traditionalists, and we have to loosen them up a bit, no matter how rigid our system. A book in which that is treated is *The Cat Ate My Gym Suit*, by Paula Danziger.

Ninth, it's a chance to make your mark, but this is done by seeing qualities in the students. That's always fun—trying to figure how you are going to get them on your team. Sometimes you have to search a long time to find a redeeming quality in a student.

Last, we're one of the few groups of people who are paid to go to school—not enough perhaps. Now let's face it, most of us liked school; that's why we're here—as long as we remember that we need to be renewed once in a while, that we need to fail and ask one another for help, that the fact that we can't stand another minute at the end of the week does not mean we will hate them on Monday. Last year I sent a questionnaire to ten of my friends—themselves fine teachers. I asked what they remembered in a great teacher. They did not say how funny or dynamic or demanding she was. They said, "she was interested in Me—Me—Me!" And it remains for us to remember that as we go to greet our classes.

XXX
Rules for Teachers

At the suggestion of my oldest child and only daughter, Mary Kate, I am attempting to put down some of the lessons and insights developed over more than thirty-five years of teaching and nearly that number of years raising a family. Most of them will be basic things and ordinary insights learned by almost every woman who has raised children in the latter part of the twentieth century, but all of them will be personal, not prescribed for others but felt deeply by the writer.

What I have come to feel most deeply is that one thing is at the heart of the success of the good teacher (and good parent—for isn't the parent finally a teacher?). One of my friends, a master teacher and award winner, answered my question of what made a great teacher by remembering one of her own. She said "she [the teacher] has to be interested in me—me—me!" And that is what the great parent is, whether the children be one in number or twelve. And "me" must be defined in terms of attention, interest, and time. Especially time.

I remember my mother in the 1940s. A superb baker of bread, with an incredible crunchy crust framing the soft white dough, she timed its exit from the oven to coincide with my return from school. There would be a fresh pot of coffee in the white enamel pot on the stove. We would sit down together and, while eating the slices of bread, still warm from the oven, she would say to me, "You know, it's very bad to eat hot bread like this. And coffee—why you're not even old enough to get ration stamps for this coffee." And then we would chat—maybe about nothing significant but that was the point. It was all significant to her if I wanted to talk about it. She gave time.

I think that is Rule Number 1: to relate to others' "Me" you must honestly give time.

Number 2 is don't worry about being personal. In a way this is a corollary of Number 1. Children are concerned about "me"; you must relate to "them." No doubt there are limits but you must be open to "them."

Number 3 is to be a good listener. This is probably an elaboration of Number 2, but it deserves being highlighted. Be open to listening in odd places—after class, in the corridor, in the kitchen unpacking the dishwasher, and, of course, when they are angry. Maybe especially when they are angry.

Number 4 is to accept your style. Find your voice and be comfortable with it. My style of lecturing has much story-telling in it. It is highly anecdotal. Early on, I wondered about it, and then I thought, "Remember you are bringing experiences as well as facts to their lives. What you say must be memorable." And then I thought back over things in my own life and thought of the people who were memorable. I realized what I remembered were stories. They were what gave life and color to my recollection of events and people. That was my style. I am sure there are others that are effective, but I firmly believe "stories"—or if you want, call them "illustrations" or "color"—are necessary to bring life to the lecture.

Number 5: Don't feel you don't know how to do something well enough. Remember Chesterton wrote that as humans we are all divine amateurs. Remember, also, the principle that some things are so worth doing they are worth doing badly. Not every pair of soiled pants I laundered was perfectly restored, nor every dinner perfectly prepared. Indeed, some were ruined.

Number 6 is don't look back. One of our friends, long ago, put it well: "You are never as bad as you feared you were, nor ever as good as you thought." In the classroom as in life.

Number 7: One of my sons said one day, "Don't nag me about this." This helped me with students later—a lot.

Number 8: Be loyal to your group—class, family, etc. Don't talk about private family matters to outsiders. Be positive in affirming their potential. Don't close doors to their aspirations. Be giving, and encourage them.

XXXI
IRELAND: 1953

Mary Jane loved Ireland. She first visited there in 1953. She returned again on our honeymoon in 1958 and with our older three children on my sabbatical in 1967. This is her account written after her return to America in 1953. It is an account she later said was "written in the romance of youth." She later saw a very changed Ireland—but as she once said, "all of us changed, not just the Irish."

She can never become just a green spot upon the tourist's itinerary. Once you've met this Lady Erin, her soft-brogued tones sing out, enticing you, as the Sirens did Ulysses, to come back to the land which is Ireland forever.

Now I know what the patriot Daniel O'Connell meant—and how he felt—about Ireland. They say that when he died he wanted his soul to rise to heaven, his heart to go to Rome, but his body to be buried in Ireland. As an American whose parents were born in the United States but whose four grandparents hailed from the "ould sod," I had always wanted to visit the land that had given to my family the old-country expressions which they preserve to this day, the easy tongue, and the unique but exasperating humor which enables them to laugh off their own troubles—and yours—as quickly as you can say "Brian Boru."

Gilbert Keith Chesterton referred to my Gaelic ancestors as the race that "God made mad, since all their wars are happy and all their songs are sad." Aside from this and other cursory descriptions, I had scant knowledge of the people of this little island which, despite pressure from within and without, has retained such a personality for itself through the ages. With twentieth-century skepticism, I thought the bogs and the leprechauns could be seen only in *Finian's Rainbow*. Now I know they are in the hearts of the Irish folk who can tell you

31 ~ Ireland: 1953

about the ghosts or "little people" which they never saw—but their "cousin's wife's sister" did. In reality, these citizens of Eire keep their feet admirably planted upon the turf and their eyes upon the realities of another world more lasting than that of fairies—or of atomic energy!

The thatched-roof cottage may be gradually disappearing, but as we drove down the coast of western Ireland, we saw many of them standing sturdily next to the "rows" of spuds, basic to Irish nutrition. These plots of farmland are neatly punctuated by stone fences which do not succeed in discouraging venturesome cows from wandering onto the narrow roads just in front of your car. They—the cows, that is—are as numerous as Irish cops on the streets of New York, and serve as a reminder that not yet have God's creatures on the "Emerald Isle" surrendered their domain to the kingship of the machine.

The little car (their pronunciation is a cross between "care" and "cyar") in which my gracious cousin had driven to Shannon airport to meet us flew along the narrow winding roads at nearly top speed—about thirty miles per hour, that is. After coming from New York to Shannon in twelve, it took us nine hours to complete the journey to Ballina, the little town in Mayo (God help us!) less than one hundred miles further along, which was our destination. These hours allowed time for frequent sidetracks, however. Life is always long enough in Ireland for folks to seize the chance to appreciate beauty when that opportunity occurs. The object of appreciation may be a geographical location, or it may be the beauty of a human relationship. As we drove along, my cousin spotted a man whom he, as an agricultural advisor, had known years before. Of course, we backed up the car, and stopped to have a visit with this Mr. O'Connor; the ruddy-faced sixty-five-year-old farmer stood with the green hills of Manor Hamilton at his back, and demonstrated the Irishman's deep appreciation of his own land.

Such visits are not the occasional but the accepted procedure in Ireland. No one, except Yankee visitors, was a bit surprised when we pulled up in front of a house which showed evidence of possessing a "wireless" later that day. One of my cousin's friends had been up for election, and James wanted to find the results. Comparatively few of the European cars being equipped with radios, he just asked the people who lived in this house if he might listen to their set for awhile. Strangers? Why they were strangers no longer!

Along the side of the road, people were digging up the turf: a certain type of hard soil, much of which is found in Ireland, providing excellent fuel against the damp chill evenings of this isle in the sea.

Every few minutes, we would encounter a patient soulful-eyed burro drawing a little cart or carrying baskets attached to his sides from one farm to another or into town to market. One morning we could hardly make our way through the streets of the Mayo town to Mass; cattle and sheep of all description occupied the main thoroughfare. Their owners, who walked or cycled alongside carrying long sticks, were bringing them to the county seat to be sold. This was a "Fair Day," and as I stole between two bulls as unobtrusively as possible, I glimpsed a bargain being concluded. Evidently a sale had just been made—the signal was a ritual of hand and fist slapping which I was to witness more than once on the streets before I left Ireland.

By the time I had spent twenty-four hours in Eire, I knew the postcards and even the fabulous scenery from the movie *The Quiet Man* were wrong. They couldn't possibly capture the view of Crough Patrick mountain where St. Patrick is supposed to have spent many days fasting. It is crowned with a little chapel to which the people of Ireland make pilgrimage on the eve of the last Sunday in July, climbing by night and receiving Holy Communion when they reach the top. Then some of them bicycle thirty or forty miles home again when they reach the bottom. Neither color movie nor water color could convey the vivid green of the grass of Shancurry, land outside the town of Drumshambo in County Leitrim where my maternal grandmother was born.

Paint brush and canvas couldn't grasp the sunset over Lough Allen or over the sea, as we watched it rise and fall at Killila Bay.

Our greatest compliment came one night when my great-aunt laughed until the tears ran down her cheeks at something we had told of our families in America. "Why," she said, "you're just like us—so plain and all." She couldn't have been as relieved as we were at this simple gesture of acceptance. We had wondered and worried about how they would feel toward the Yankees who had flown over. Now everything was all right. The peat fire burned brighter, and no one minded that the Irish rain beat heavily down upon the pieces of turf stacked neatly outside the door, set aside to be dried for fuel on future damp evenings. The pot of "spuds" still hung over the open blaze; Uncle Mick was smoking the pipe my father had sent to his grandmother's youngest brother. (We hoped he wouldn't notice that it was made in England!) We had been telling the story of how our grandmother had come over as a very young girl, seventy years before, arriving at the little town in Illinois where her uncle lived. She had been greeted by a man with a buggy who said, "Are you Cronin's greenhorn?" Now as we laughed together, they knew we had not come to Ireland to look for bathtubs (and 'twas a good thing we didn't!), but were sincerely interested in getting to know them. By now we knew that we wanted terribly for them to like us.

Their eyes, that evening, reflecting the welcome blaze, said we were accepted. Their gestures reiterated it in the way they got out fiddle and accordion and tried to teach us the Irish Half-Set. I wanted to learn that dance that night as I have never wanted to pick up a Samba or a new Fox Trot Twist. We answered it in the way we tried, unutterably clumsy at first, to learn the dance steps that night on the concrete in western Ireland.

We had tea with them that night. This is the brew which is served a minimum of three times a day. If you don't believe it, just try to get a morning cup of coffee in some spots of rural Eire. The final meal of the day, however, employs the word "Tea" as its title and includes a variety of edibles, but always soda bread at least. In comparison, our breads would seem half-baked to an Irishman—to any European, for that matter. Actually, soda bread is of a different consistency and recipe than regular yeast bread and in some localities of Ireland it is baked over the open fire inside a Dutch oven. We horrified our hosts, at first, by our drinking of tea "black." They worried about our abstemiousness in drinking tea without milk or sugar, a practice which they carried out, they said, only on Ash Wednesday and Good Friday.

Withal, one is aware that Ireland in 1953 faces a galaxy of problems. To obscure them in the Irish mist would be like disregarding termites which are eating away at the very fibre—or bog, if you prefer—of a small but great country.

Late marriages are blamed as reason enough for what some feel is an alarming decline of the population. Others retort that given proper interpretation, statistics would tell a different story; they say that the population is not now decreasing in any alarming manner. However, many of the young people feel they must look elsewhere than Ireland—often to England or America—for any professional or job opportunities, and this situation could not be conducive to a high marriage rate within Ireland. One old woman spoke of marriage in one's twenties as a bit "wild"; this attitude perhaps reflects the idiosyncrasy of age, but would be more laughable if it were being contradicted in practice every day.

The reasons for late marriages must be as varied as the localities in Ireland; certainly it would be hard to generalize on the matter. However, one wonders, seeing the limited land and more limited cash in parts of rural Eire, just how the son of a family would make a living for a wife and where they would live, if he were to "pop the question." Certainly, the attitude of a man in Ireland toward taking a wife would be in direct contrast to that of my itinerant worker friend in America who proposed to the girl of his choice by asking her to share in his life. After all, his car did have a rumble seat! In a country where the matchmaker, the formal courtship, and the dowry are a thing of the not-too-distant past, this would hardly be a popular attitude. Several factors, then, plus the great migration of large numbers of young Irish people would be enough to make any marriage rate sink.

The backwardness of whole rural areas of Ireland in regard to progressive methods of farming and living is often decried. Ireland being limited in natural resources, the present Irish government tries to stimulate and encourage the farmer to plant trees, build fences, and drain land by bearing the substantial burden of such expense. One alert and well-informed couple whom we met feel that individual resourcefulness and initiative are stifled by the way this is being done. They think that the Irish farmer has become like the man who, when he falls into a ditch, waits for the hand which has always pulled him out of it before. With each repetition of this process, his muscles become flabbier until one day he no longer has the strength to extricate himself from a ditch when help is not to be had.

One little lady who spoke to us on the street of Ballina said she had us picked out for Yankees from the very first time she glimpsed our white hats and bright colors. We wondered if she knew that our combinations of colors was especially bright because we were wearing all our sweaters for extra warmth against the damp cold. This woman asked, "What happens to those who 'go out to America' that they forget those at home so easily?" I wanted to tell her they didn't. I wanted to say that the number of people I had met in her own country who had been "out" and had then come back to live in Eire was living testimony that an Irishman does not easily forget his land and his people.

In fact, real Irishmen the world over suffer from a peculiar kind of heart trouble. They have the kind of hearts which can stand the Irish Half-Set at seventy-two, a dance which would put our middle-aged golf or tennis athletes on the bench in five minutes. But the disease that puts a pain in the chest of an Irishman is one that anyone who has watched the crowds flock to a St. Patrick's Day Mass in New York or Chicago can understand. It comes from an attachment to faith and land which is deep within the Irish heart. Allegiance to the isle rising out of the sea, which is Ireland, is loyalty to the land baptized by St. Patrick, not merely to a geographical location. It is a love of the greatness of the Patricks, the Brigids, the Columkilles, of the heroic standards of the isle of saints and scholars, and of those minds and hearts which can pen—and believe—words like Joseph Plunkett's "I see His blood upon the rose." It is fidelity to something much deeper than the orange, white, and green flag; it is loyalty to a heritage of Faith and fight. The term "vanishing Irish" has been bandied about, with many pros and cons, a great deal in recent years. I have made no exhaustive survey of the country; I have spent some unforgettable days in Ireland. Somehow, I feel that the country to whose symbols so many heartstrings are attached cannot easily sink into the sea— not, at least, without a mighty big splash.

XXXII
Marge Callahan at Play

"So most of all, Peggy, it's being what you want to be in life that makes you happy," concluded Marge Callahan, putting down her hair brush and looking at the grimacing face behind her in the mirror. Although she didn't have her glasses on and the light there was bad, Marge was pretty sure that Peggy had "turned her off."

"She's gone again," Marge thought, and added mentally "as always." But she said instead, "O.K., hon, you can read a while before you go to bed." And she got the usual appreciative hug as Peggy scooted back to her room. "I wonder why I always end up lecturing her," Marge mused, "but darn it—she needs it." Peggy had bubbled in earlier that evening, asking if she could get one of those psychedelic skirts that her friends Beth and Martha had. They wanted to dress just alike. "Oh why is she so groupy? Why can't she be her own girl? There I am lecturing her again, even when she's not here," Marge laughed.

Marge wondered how Jim would have handled the matter of the skirts. He seemed to take Peggy's notions less seriously than she did. "I know what you're worried about, hon," he would say, "but other thirteen-year-old kids are going to pot parties and such. Don't lean so hard on Peggy. It's natural for her to want to be like her friends at this age. If those three girls want to put on identical skirts and walk down the street looking like three peas in a pod, let them."

But it bothered her, and it should bother Jim, she thought. As a lawyer working often in juvenile court, he saw more than his share of girls who wanted to be "just like the next one." Then Marge had to chuckle in spite of herself. "What a dreadful prig I sound." She sat down to write some letters before Jim would come home, looking forward eagerly to that time even after fourteen years. Peggy did, too, and when her father worked late, she usually detained him for a minute as he passed her room. "Funny," she thought, "how those two always seemed to have a special understanding, even in the days when I would go off, leaving him with a tiny Peggy, a pile of diapers, and two extra pins which he said he needed for security. The two boys a few years later were much harder for him to take, with their 'that's mine' and 'he hit me' at predictable intervals."

The front door clicked. Marge listened. He would be looking over his mail, and that chuckle would be for Tommy's first-grade paper with its triumphant star and his teacher's simple but eloquent "You've made it with the A's, Tommy. Now full speed ahead to the B's." Now here he was coming up the stairs, and she decided that she'd forget the psychedelic skirt for tonight.

The next day Marge had a call from Mrs. Bowman, Beth's mother, about filling in for bridge. She declined and hoped Beth's mother really believed that she didn't know how to play. Martha came in with Peggy after school. "Would you like Mom to pick you up for the Mother's Club meeting tomorrow, Mrs. Callahan? I told her that Peggy's dad would be away on the business trip with the car." "Oh, I'm not going to the meeting tomorrow Martha. I have a lot of papers to read for that adult education class I'm teaching at the high school. This is the week I promised to have the papers back."

Marge thought she caught a look from Peggy, but she wasn't sure. "Oh well," she comforted herself, "the talk is on flower-arranging, something I couldn't learn if I went to a hundred meetings." Besides, those two hours in the afternoon when Peggy and Tommy were at school and Jimmy went to kindergarten were such a bonanza. "I need them," she told herself again, "to do those papers." Besides that, what was the use of reading papers and evaluating other people's creative writing if you didn't do some yourself?

On Friday Peggy said that she didn't feel like going to play practice after school. She asked when her father would be home, and Marge answered quickly, "Oh, not until Tuesday, Peg. You asked me that yesterday. What's up?" "Oh, there was something I wanted to talk over with him," Peggy answered. Marge covered the slight annoyance in her voice when she said, "Won't I do?" The answer came swiftly. "Well, it's about this play we're giving." Peggy plunged on, encouraged by Marge's non-committal silence. "You always think that

I'm doing things because the other kids do—like the skirts. But it's not that at all this time. I know I started in this drama group because Beth and Martha were doing it, but . . . . Well . . . . This play is good, really good, and you won't even come to it."

It all came out in a rush and Peggy—Peggy, of all people—started to cry. "Why Peggy, what ever do you mean?" Marge was talking to the large mound of girl now crumpled in her lap. "Have you ever, ever, ever been in any kind of performance at school that I didn't come to?" "But, this is at a Mother's Club meeting, and you don't like them. You think they're silly." "Did I ever say that?" "No, but you looked it when Beth asked if you wanted to have her mother pick you up for the meeting on flower-arranging." "Oh, Peggy, that's because it was about flower-arranging, and I'm so awful with my hands. I never thought you'd think . . . ."

But Peggy was sunny again, hugging her and saying, "Then you'll come?" And she was gone, with a flurry of skirt and short curly hair, calling over her shoulder, "That's what I wanted to talk to Dad about. I wanted him to get you to come."

It worried Marge a bit that Peg hadn't come right to her, instead wanting to approach her through her father. And she resolved not to be so disapproving after this. When Jim came home on Tuesday and she told him the story, he laughed. "I think I'd better go away oftener. You and Peggy seem to get together more when I'm not on hand." It all seemed to be solved. Marge would go to the Mother's Club meeting at which Peggy was to be in a play. Then the complication occurred. The president called on Friday to ask Marge if she would like to talk to the next meeting. "To be perfectly frank," she finally said, "I'm asking you this late because Mrs. Crane from the *Times* was to speak on remaining a creative and feminine woman though competing in the professional world. Well, Mrs. Crane's mother became ill and she left on the morning plane for Atlanta. I thought you might do something in the other direction, like 'How to Maintain Interest in the Professional World Though Staying at Home' or something like that."

Marge was silent for a moment. She recalled Peggy's face the night she had blurted out "You never go!" She *had* to go this time, and if she was to be there anyway at the meeting, how could she refuse the

32 – Marge Callahan at Play

woman's request. She couldn't, of course. So Marge half-heartedly agreed to give the talk.

All the time Marge Callahan prepared her talk, she was bothered. It wasn't the fact that she was their second choice. Marge had been an organizational program chairman once herself, and she knew how hard it was when someone failed an assignment. It was really that she couldn't understand why they were having a play and a talk at the same time. But she was hardly in a position to ask about the matter of either Peggy or the Mother's Club lady. "I'll bet they don't give the girls credit for being able to carry the whole program," she thought with irritation, remembering all the while that she had no idea what Peggy and her friends might be preparing. But Marge knew she had to accept and she had to be there to see Peggy's play, and there it was.

On the day of the program, Marge had her hair done, hoping it wouldn't look too beauty-parlorish, and dressed very carefully. Immediately upon her arrival, Mrs. Windsor brought her to the front row of the auditorium and explained apologetically that the moderator of the girls' drama club had asked if they might include their play in the program. This would be given first, not because it was the more important part of the afternoon, but because she thought it would be good to "take care of the children first." Marge wished feverishly that she would go away, but when she didn't, Marge volunteered that she had heard that the drama group was very interesting and added, almost aggressively, that her daughter was in this play and that it was an important reason for her being there. The president said, "Oh!" as if it had meaning, and returned to the podium. Marge moved back with Beth's mother and they settled down to wait for their girls.

It was a modern-day *Tempest*, with Peggy as Prospero and Beth as Miranda. Instead of the island to which Prospero fled in Shakespeare's play, this Prospero lived in a lone farmhouse outside Philadelphia. He was not the nobleman-scholar whose lieutenants had been disloyal to him, but the sensitive man who had found his society rotten. It became gradually, gracefully evident that Prospero was black, and he had fled with his daughter because he did not want her to experience the suffering of exclusion by the white race or the trauma of great militancy from the black. So he planned to raise her completely apart from all sociological tensions.

You got a bit of Shakespeare's wisdom as it went along, but a lot of it was someone else—and a fairly good someone else. Marge found herself wondering how they were going to come to the reconciliation part. She remembered that at the end of the *Tempest* they were all friends. All was forgiven and Prospero was returned to his people.

Just then the curtain came down on the scene and there was the president again at her side, a little annoyed that Marge had gotten away from that nice front seat where she had placed her. Marge listened in complete amazement to what the lady was saying, but before she could retort, the president was halfway up the aisle to say it to everybody. Almost unbelieving, Marge heard her say carefully and tactfully that everyone was enjoying the lovely play, but there was another part of the program planned. Perhaps the girls could have the second part of the play at the next meeting.

Marge was aghast. She pulled herself to her full height—every quarter-inch of that five-feet-eight was there. She rushed up the aisle, and to the astonishment of the somewhat crestfallen stage crew, she called, "Stop!" They set down the scenery they were already moving, and watched Mrs. Callahan as she took the microphone a bit too firmly from the club president. "I believe I am the other part of the program, and I'm supposed to talk about being professional and creative. Well, let me tell you, I've not heard anything more creative than this play today. Whoever did this little takeoff on Shakespeare is telling us more about being creative than any million words I might say. And I, for one, want to hear the end." They heard no more of what she had to say, for they were all clapping in thunderous agreement. In a minute Marge was sitting down again and the curtain was raised for Act II.

She had wondered how they solved the reconciliation thing, and it was left a little up in the air. Mr. Simmons, also Prospero, decided to come back to Philadelphia and work for the rights of minorities, when he discovered his daughter was becoming only a spectator. He knew she had to care about people and problems, and when a man whom he had worked with before asked him to come back for a particularly tough job, he came. After the play, the audience called for the author, and to Marge's shock, there stood Peggy, red and wobbly. But then she smiled radiantly, and in that moment it seemed to Marge that she grew up. She said—she actually said—that if it hadn't been for the help of Miss Downers, the moderator, and the inspiration of her mother, she couldn't have done it.

Marge and Peggy refused all the offers of a ride home. After they had together thanked all the people—mothers, students, and a few teachers—for the kind words they were saying about Peggy's production, they started the six-block walk home. Peggy told Marge all about the terrible time she had had not asking her help or advice on this play, because she wanted to do it herself. "I was afraid you'd just write it, Mom. But everyone knows you can do it. I've got to show that I can." Mother and daughter walked arm in arm, silently for a while, until Marge threw up her hands in horror. "Oh, Peggy, I never said a thing to that president. What ever will she think of me, cutting off the second part of her program and then leaving without a word?" But Peggy was laughing, "I explained to her, Mom, that you didn't know a thing about my writing the play when you said that everyone wanted to see the rest of it. I loved the way you did that, Mom. You didn't care how it sounded. You said it because you thought it was right. It reminded me of what you always say—'It's not what people expect of you in life; it's being what you want to be in life that's important.'"

"That does sound familiar," laughed Marge. "And so does that," answered Peggy, as they turned the corner and heard Tommy and Jimmy beating on the back door and yelling, "Let us in Mother. We know you're home." Yes, she was home, Marge thought, in a way she never had been before.

XXXIII
Dear Teacher*

Miss Grogan, *until recently supervisor of Girls' Activities for the Chicago Archdiocesan CYO, is now an instructor of English at St. Francis Xavier College for Women, Chicago.*

My seams were straight, my skirt was smooth and my hair was newly waved. I was sure of these details and wished I could be as confident about the reliability of my face and my knees. I wondered, sitting in the crowded auditorium, if they revealed the apprehension I felt as the principal's list of introductions dwindled. In a minute now she would come to me, the youngest and newest of the lay teachers. As I heard her crisply announce my name and then the names of the fated students who would be under my guidance during this first year on the blackboard side of the desk, my heart registered a combination of thrill and dread. Both feelings were later proved to be fully justified.

I learned a lot during that first year as does any novice teacher, partly from her own many mistakes, partly from those older and wiser around her—and mostly from her students. One of the last-mentioned met me three years later and identified herself thus: "Do you remember me? I'm Marita Connell; I was in that class that broke you in." And little did she know how literally true that was!

Teacher Learns

I learned the usual and most necessary lessons of how to maintain discipline and how to give assignments within measurable distance

---

* Editor's Note: In later years, Mary Jane laughingly referred to this essay (which originally appeared in the September 1, 1956 edition of *America*) as a "period piece," outdated by the religious and educational turmoil of the 1960s and 1970s. Perhaps. But beyond its content the article perfectly displays her enthusiasm toward the career she loved so much. It describes the beginning of Mary Jane's teaching career, which makes it an appropriate place to conclude her essays.

of the amount of work you can correct. I learned also that the lay teacher in the Catholic school occupies a somewhat unstructured position in the world of her profession and in the world of her students. Just what that position is to be depends upon her attitude and her use of the power she is given.

Because she does not wear the religious garb of the order in whose school she teaches, there will be a certain group of young people who do not think her deserving of the respect they give to a religious teacher. A private and non-belligerent chat with such a student, after school hours when none of her friends are around to "watch Judy get called in," often brings forth the deeply rooted reverence for authority which is present in almost every child reared in a Catholic home and school. After such a talk, one girl left with a new feeling, even about herself. She had heard a few things about the dignity of human beings and the respect due to them. She had been introduced to the idea that the power and authority of a teacher are not for the glory of her who governs but rather for the sake of the governed.

My students were all girls, high-school juniors. When we discussed careers, many of them wondered and asked frankly why I had chosen "this one." At first my reaction was defensive because I resented the way they said "this one," until I remembered that at sixteen or seventeen almost every experience is met vicariously. They were potential stewardesses or nurses or secretaries or lady politicians or even teachers, and they were honestly interested in knowing, not how "one" chooses, but how I, a person whom they knew, had chosen a field of work. I was glad I could tell them there was a kind of glamor as well as a purpose in teaching. There was the challenge of having infinitely wonderful human beings to whom I had full truth to offer, and the adventure of never quite knowing what one day was going to bring in the way of good or bad.

That matter of the "full truth" is pretty important. As a teacher in a Catholic school, I had the advantage of imparting knowledge as important as the meaning of life itself and as true as the Source of that life. Here was a philosophy of man which recognized that he is a creature created by God, fallen in Adam but gloriously redeemed by Christ. Each day, as I taught, new implications of these realities came to me and I felt sorry for my friends, who were struggling in some cases with a philosophy of education which takes into consideration only a part of man's nature.

Here I had my own class and the chance to plant, sow, and, once in a while, reap. Those classmates of mine, as they went from school to school on a substitute basis during their first semester of teaching, were learning that versatility and quick adjustment were necessary for survival. I was learning other things which made that year's experience valuable; for instance, that, when truths long known are to be conveyed to others, one must relearn them. In making a play of Shakespeare intriguing to teen-agers, I sometimes discovered a richness within it which I had never sensed.

That brings me to the question which I must have answered a hundred times during the three years I spent at that Catholic school. "And how do you like working for the nuns?" I found it splendid. The generosity that is characteristic of their giving of themselves to the life of the spirit doesn't stop when they face their fellow worker, whether that co-worker happens to be wearing a black habit or a red wool suit. It's there and it is felt.

"How Do You Like It?"

There is warmth in the response "I'd love to" from the little nun who runs off your tests on the convent dittograph machine. The sister cook who wants to know if "those girls" have enough to eat is really concerned. The older teachers are ready and willing to discuss with you, step by step, the day's program, though they've been through it umpteen times—never letting on that they might have been "assigned" by Mother Superior to do this very job.

These were just the background of a real opportunity for exchange of ideas and stimulating discussion of school problems with women who were both professionals and religious. At our academy, lay teachers definitely had a voice in the business of the school, some of which was conducted at faculty meetings held biweekly after class hours. This spirit of unified working *with* rather than *for* was carried through, and even if we might be called Maureen or Mary Jane when the students weren't around, our decisions regarding matters which came under our domain were respected and supported.

Though there was this family unity among the teachers, we lay teachers heard more than our share of students' gripes, and in these informal out-of-class conversations we were sometimes handed more serious matters. You discovered a lot of things about these fresh and lovely young girls whose faces bore not a line; their lives were not always so happy and unfurrowed. Scratch the surface a bit and serious problems were occasionally revealed. They told lay teachers things they might not tell the nuns, for they felt you were dealing with some of the same temptations they had to fight. Your role was sometimes to listen, another time to refer them to a confessor or spiritual advisor, and occasionally to counsel.

Students absorb teachers' attitudes and reactions to events, I had been told, and now I saw it happen a hundred times a day. In September, I complained to a priest who had been one of my college professors that I had taught something poorly and he consoled me with a remark like this: "I hate to tell you, but most of the time those teenagers are studying not so much the material you are giving them as you." At that time it was a frightening thought; by June I was sure it was true.

One of the main things which resulted consciously from that year was a feeling of belonging to something truly great. It had been a struggle, to be sure. For instance, you were pretty sick before you ever stayed home, because you knew there was no one to take your place. But you had been trusted with an opportunity to reach young minds and hearts, and you had grown deeper and larger—as well as tired—because of it.

Today I hear and I agree that Catholic schools need to give more thought to benefits, to pensions, to tenure, and some of them to recognizing the lay teachers as an integral part of the Catholic school faculty, not as extras whom they would like to replace with a nun any day. They need to make real efforts to increase salaries according to the local scale of wages and prices. It is necessary to the happiness and well-being of the devoted teachers they employ and to the schools' own existence.

But I believe, also, that anyone who thinks mainly of salary and benefits as the chief means of drawing lay teachers to the Catholic school is misdirecting his attention. At best, the Catholic schools' ability to pay will always be slightly behind that of public tax-supported systems. There is a stronger appeal than wages, and one that has yet to be given full credit and use. It lies in bringing to young college graduates the news of the opportunities that await them in the Catholic school to share the treasures which their liberal educations have given them. It consists in showing them that here is a chance to respond to the invitation of the Great Teacher to "go and teach" in His name.

MORTALITY *is but the Stuff you wear*
To show the better on the imperfect sight.
Your home is surely with the changeless light
Of which you are the daughter and the heir.
For as you pass, the natural life of things
Proclaims the Resurrection : as you pass
Remembered summer shines across the grass
And somewhat in me of the immortal sings.

You were not made for memory, you are not
Youth's accident I think but heavenly more ;
Moulding to meaning slips my pen's poor blot
And opening wide that long forbidden door
    Where stands the Mother of God, your exemplar.
    How beautiful, how beautiful you are !

                                  Hilaire Belloc, *Sonnet V*

INDEX

Editor's Note: This index seeks to be reasonably comprehensive but not exhaustive. For example, it does not catalogue the references to family members or, for the most part, to friends, on the theory that the user of the index is likely to be interested in the book primarily for the cultural and sociological insights that it may afford.

Abel, D. Herbert, 61
Academy of Our Lady, 9, 16, 19, 35, 45, 47-50, 51, 54, 56, 66-67, 69, 70-73, 75, 77, 78, 79-80, 83, 112, 222, 246-50 (see also School Sisters of Notre Dame)
America, 82, 246
Andrea Doria, 71
Archdiocesan Council of Catholic Men, 77
Auburn Foods and Liquor, 106
Auburn Park Branch Library, 23

Bacon, Francis, 212
Barbie Dolls, 215-16
Baseball Hall of Fame, 44
Beatty, Warren, 76
Belloc, Hilaire, xii, 138-39
Bening, Annette, 76
Bettelheim, Bruno, 214
Beverly Branch Library, 137
Beverly Community Nursery School, 119, 124-25, 127, 131
Bismarck Hotel, 33
Bonwit Teller, 8, 60, 92
Bryant, Rev. Thomas J., S.J., 91
Bud Billiken Parade, 51

Cabbage Patch Dolls, 215-16
Cameron, Ann, 213
Campion Hall, Oxford, 129
Campion High School, 44-46, 52
Cantigny, 88
Capitol Theater, 14, 19, 24
Captain Kangaroo, 196-97
Carrabine, Rev. Martin, S.J., 49, 52-53, 91, 98
Carson Pirie Scott & Co., 111, 127, 134, 174

Carson's Men's Grill, 126
Catholic Charities, 98
Catholic Worker, 52-53
Catholic Youth Organization (CYO), 77-80, 81-82, 246
Chada, Joseph, 94, 108
Chapin, Harry, 205, 224-26
Chesterton, G.K., 72, 194-95, 233, 234
Chicago Daily News, 50, 134
Chicago Granitine Manufacturing Company, xiii, 3-6, 19, 21, 27, 31, 38, 41, 52, 53, 96, 100, 169, 172, 189, 199
Chicago Inter-Student Catholic Action (CISCA), 49-50, 51, 52, 54, 91
Chicago State University, 134 (see also Chicago Teachers College)
Chicago Sun-Times, 206, 216, 218, 220, 223
Chicago Teachers College, 94-95, 97, 107, 108, 111, 125, 134, 185
Chicago Tribune, 79, 88
Chicago, University of, 68, 82
Chicago White Sox, 224
Children's Memorial Hospital, 121
Clinton, Hillary, 125
Civic Opera House, 50, 54
Clark, Gen. Mark, 95
Clark Street Streetcar, 14, 20, 21, 40
Cogley, John, 49
Comiskey Park, 76
Commonwealth Edison, 49
Coughlin, Rev. Charles, 13, 183
Courtney, Thomas, 5
Cowan, Ray, 93
Craven, John, 112-13

D'Arcy, Rev. Martin, S.J., 128-29
Daley, Richard, 83
Danziger, Paula, 231

253

Day, Dorothy, 50, 52-53
Dennis, Patrick, 198
DePaul University, 78
Dever, Joe, 82
Dickens, Charles, 29, 33
Doherty, Eddie, 50
Dollard, Rev. Stewart E., S.J., 100
Dominican House of Studies, 83
Doyle Center, 61
Doyle, Rev. Charles, S.J., 61, 77, 91
Drovers Bank, 55
Dunne, Sam, 113-14
Durkin, Martin, 33

Egan, Rev. John, 75, 76
Eisenhower, Dwight D., 33
Eliot, T.S., 208
English, Rev. Mike, 91
Ets, Marie Hall, 213
Evergreen Plaza, 111, 127

Fair Store, 44
Finnegan, Rev. William A., S.J., 91
Fischer, Dr. William, 99
Fleming, Dr. Arthur, 106, 108
Fluornoy, Valerie, 214
Frank's Department Store, 14, 23
Friendship House, 50
Frisbie, Margery, 75, 76

Gallagher, Rev. Ralph, S.J., 60
Ganss, Rev. George, S.J., 56
Garden Cab Company, 101
Gerrietts, John, 100, 152
Ginocchio Bros., 33
Gladstone, Joe, 78
Glass Menagerie, 17, 62
Gobreski, Matt, 77-79
Goodman Theater, 111
Granada Theater, 95, 205, 224
Greeley, Rev. Andrew, 74, 76
Greene, Graham, 48, 50, 230
Gresham School, 24
Gross, Calvin, 134
Guardian Angel, 86
Guest, Edgar, 170

Harrington, Ann, 50
Hart, Dr. Cecil, 130-31
Hayes, John, 77-78
Hesburgh, Rev. Theodore, C.S.C., 225
Hines Hospital, 88
Hirsch, E.D., 230
Hirsch High School, 67-69
Hoffman, Rev. Kenneth, 71
Hogan, Rev. Joseph F., S.J., 58-61, 70, 77-78, 89, 91
Holy Name Cathedral, 60, 122
Holy Name Societies, 78
Hopkins, Gerard Manley, 61, 67, 71, 230
Hueck, Catherine de, 50
Hummel, Bertha, 92
Hunt, Irene, 231
Hutchins, Robert M., 68

Illinois Catholic Club for Women, 58, 59
Integrity, 50

Jackson, Carol, 50
James, Henry, 136
Jewish Daily Forward, The, 229
John A. Colby & Sons Co., 115
John Carroll University, 85, 86, 88, 89, 91, 94
Johnson, Lyndon, 120
Johnston, Rev. Charles, OP, 91
Jordan, Dixie, 107

Keats, John, 211
Keeley Brewery, 26
Keeshan, Bob, 196-97
Kelly, Msgr. Edward, 77
Kennedy, Caroline, 120
Kennedy, Jacqueline, 120
Kennedy, John F., 120
Kent, Gene, 77-78
Kingston, Maxine Hong, 213
Kresge's, 15

"L" (Chicago), 21, 24, 58, 86-87, 108, 126, 133-34, 179
L'Engle, Madeleine, 229

Index

Landers, Ann, 229-30
Lane, Dr. Robert, 99, 101, 108, 116, 121
le Blanc, Mariette, 60
Leo High School, 46, 95
Lewis, Frank J., 58
Lewis, Julia Deal, 58
Lewis University, 134
Lietz, Paul, 89
Little Company of Mary Hospital, 126-27
Longwood, see Academy of Our Lady
Longwood Cenacle, 91, 123, 126
Longwood News, 49
Loop (Chicago), 13-15, 21, 33-34, 133-34
Lord, Bette Bao, 213
Loyola Academy, 77
Loyola University, 7, 17, 46, 56-57, 58-61, 66-67, 70, 71, 72, 75-76, 77-78, 84, 87, 89, 91, 94, 95, 96, 98, 99, 100, 111, 124, 126, 128-29, 133, 152, 222
Lucas, Mary Ehrie, 83-84

Macbeth, 66, 72, 222, 228
Malcak, Tony, 78-79, 81, 85
Maritain, Jacques, 48
Marquette High School, 56
Marquette University, 54-57, 61, 94, 134
Marshall Field's, 8, 14, 15, 34, 100-01, 133-34, 217
Martin D'Arcy Art Gallery, 129
Maurin, Peter, 52
Maxwell Street, xiii, 13, 16, 21
McCarthy, Mary, xi
McCormick, Robert R., 88
Mercy Home for Boys (also known as Working Boys Home), 77-78, 88
Mercy Hospital, 99
Metropolitan Life, 10, 11, 22
Molloy, Msgr. Patrick J., 75-76, 91
Montgomery Ward's, 60
Morgan Park Academy, 83, 122, 123-24, 131
Morgan Park Military Academy, 123

Morrison Hotel, 33
Mount Mary College, 54, 81, 84
Mulholland, Clem, 112
Mulholland Real Estate, 112
Mundelein College, 54
Mundelein, George Cardinal, 75
Murphy, Morgan, 49
Mutual National, 23

National College of Education/National-Louis University, 72, 134, 137, 155, 158, 222
Natov, Roni, 213
Newberry Library, 17, 84-85, 86, 95
Northwestern University, 132, 224
Notre Dame, University of, 20, 132, 134, 157, 168, 224-26

O'Brien, George, 106
O'Connell, Daniel, 234
O'Gara, James, 49
Oak Lawn Library, 137
Old San Hotel, 45

Packard Motor Car Company, 29-30, 34, 40-41
Paderewski, Ignace Jan, 40
Palmer House, 33, 86
Parishes
 Christ the King, 76
 St. Barnabas, 118, 121, 124
 St. Carthage, 98
 St. John the Baptist, 4, 37
 St. Leo (Church and School), 19-21, 26, 42, 46, 47, 74-76, 91-93, 104, 168, 182-84
 St. Margaret of Scotland, 124
 St. Mary's, 126
 St. Rita, 32
 St. Sabina, 76
 St. Walter, 97
 Visitation, 4, 76
Passavant Hospital, 130
Pestalozzi-Froebel Teachers College, 133-34
Polacco, Patricia, 214
Poor Clare Sisters, 7-9, 173

Pope John XXIII, 116
Pope Pius XII, 92

Reader's Digest, 48
Reagan, Nancy, 8
Reichert, Dr. John L., 109-10
Repplier, Agnes, 50
Restaurants
    Balducci's, 10-11
    Berghoff, 79, 111, 134
    Cavallini's, 107
    E.W. Rieck's Beanery, 14-15
    Lander's, 86
    Mario's, 86
    Oak Lawn, 137
    Old Cathay, 60-61
    Ranch, 60
    Yonkers, 60
Ridge Country Club, 131
Riverview, 46
Rock Island Train, 134, 177, 194
Roosevelt, Eleanor, 13
Roosevelt, Franklin D., 13
Rubicam, Charles, 17, 39
Rubicam's Business College/Roofing Company, 10, 17, 39, 52, 62-65, 71

St. Anne, 91, 94
St. Anthony, 34
St. Augustine, 119
St. Clare, 7
St. Edmund Campion, 44 (see also Campion)
St. Francis, 7
St. Ignatius Grade School, 77
St. Ignatius High School/College Prep, 83, 95, 122, 131-32
St. Mary of the Lake Seminary, 75
St. Mary's College (Ind.), 20
St. Mary's Hospital (Mo.), 88-89
St. Mary's School (Wis.), 45
St. Patrick, 4, 38, 102, 104, 169, 189, 236, 239
St. Peter's Church, 34, 134, 179
St. Valentine, 198-200
St. Xavier College, 48-49, 81-85, 87, 91, 93, 94, 96, 120, 122, 246

San Souci, Robert, 213
Sanfield, Steve, 214
Scalia, Antonin, 138
School Sisters of Notre Dame, 9, 45, 47-50, 54, 83, 246-50 (see also Academy of Our Lady and Mount Mary College)
    Charitas, 48
    Claude, 48
    Ewald, 48, 49, 56, 71
    Fortunata, 73
    Francele, 71
    Francine, 48
    Mary Chrysostom, 81
    Mary Hester Valentine, 9, 16, 48, 49-50, 52, 84-85, 86, 95, 230
    Mechtilde, 56
    Mona, 72
    Philemon, 50
    Seraphia Marie, 73
    Theodora, 70, 73, 246
    Theresita, 49
Sears Roebuck, 14, 40, 78, 112, 230
Service Master, 115
Shakespeare, William, 66, 72, 82, 189, 193, 207-08, 222, 228, 230, 243-44, 248
Shamrock Beauty Parlor, 51-52
Sheil, Bishop Bernard J., 78
Sheil School of Social Studies, 78
Sheldon School, 97
Shewbridge Field, 20, 44, 46
Shewbridge, Msgr. Peter F., 13, 20, 44, 46, 74-75, 183
Siena High School, 82
Sisters of Mercy, 48, 49, 81, 120 (see also Siena High School and St. Xavier College)
    Anacleta, 83
    Antonine, 83, 122
    Benoit, 82
    Consilia, 82
    Josetta Butler, 81-82
    Mary of the Angels, 83
Sisters of Providence, 42, 47, 74-75 (see also St. Leo)
    Irma Therese, 47, 74

Index

Social Justice, 13, 183
Society of Jesus (Jesuits), see Campion High School and Loyola University as well as individual entries for various priests
Sousa, John Philip, 47
South Bend Tribune, 226
South Shore Country Club, 76, 91, 146-48
Spaeth, Dr. Ralph, 109-10, 124, 126, 129
Spargo, John Webster, 67
Statler Hotel, 53
Stevens Hotel, 33
Stratman, Rev. Carl, C.S.V., 17-18, 92
Summerdale Police Scandal, 109
Surtz, Rev. Edward, S.J., 67, 92, 94
Sutherland School, 131
Swift, Jonathan, 209

Techny, 37-38
Tempest, 243-44
Time, 56
Today, 49
Trinity College, 24
Truman, Harry, 54

Valentine, Mary Hester, S.S.N.D., see School Sisters of Notre Dame
Viorst, Judith, 227
Visitation High School, 24

Walgreen Mansion, 123
Wall Street Journal, 179
Washington Square Park, 84
Water Tower Place, 58
Waugh, Evelyn, 128-29, 230
Wesley Memorial Hospital, 87-88, 98, 108, 109, 121
Weyand, Rev. Norman, S.J., 61, 67, 71, 84, 128-29
Widener University School of Law, 134
Wieboldt's, 14, 40
Williams, Charles, 133
Williams, Tennessee, 17, 62, 217
Wolff, Joe, 61

Woolworth's, 15
Working Boys Home, see Mercy Home for Boys
Works Progress Administration (WPA), 5

Xavierite, 82, 83, 93, 94

Yale Daily News, 55
Yale University, 55, 132, 136, 153
Y.W.C.A., 10